THE
MUSTARD
SEED
BOOK

THE
MUSTARD
SEED
BOOK

GROWING FAITH
IN YOUR OWN BACKYARD

MIKE FLYNN

Chosen Books

A Division of Baker Book House Co
Grand Rapids, Michigan 49516

Published by Chosen Books
a division of Baker Book House Company
P.O. Box 6287, Grand Rapids, MI 49516-6287

Printed in the United States of America

Library of Congress Cataloging-in-Publication Data

Flynn, Mike, 1940–
   The mustard seed book : growing faith in your own backyard / Mike Flynn.
     p. cm.
   Includes bibliographical references.
   ISBN 0-8007-9228-9
   1. Faith. 2. Spiritual life—Christianity. I. Title.
   BV4637.F56   1995
   234'.2—dc20

                                       94-40868

To my wife, Sue,

I offer to you this handful of grain
Sickled and chaff'd, sometimes with pain
You have believed! a thousand times strong
I exult in your grace and laud you this song.

Contents

Acknowledgments

I wish to thank the congregations I have served in these last twenty-five years, for they have shown me true faith: Immanuel Episcopal Church, El Monte, California, and St. Jude's Episcopal Church, Burbank, California. To Doug Gregg and Rowena Phillips and Jane Campbell, my editor, I give thanks for your friendship and helpful and corrective critiques.

Part 1
God's Reasons for Faith

1
God's Stake in Our Faith

Once when Jesus was giving a teaching on prayer, He concluded His remarks with this question: "When the Son of Man comes, will he find faith on the earth?" (Luke 18:8). For a moment Jesus leapfrogged way into the future, fore-seeing the day at the end of the age when He would return to earth. As His gaze went to that distant day, He realized that what He would be looking for on His return was faith.

Why? What is so important about having faith? That is the question we want to look at in this book.

As I have traveled around and taught in the Christian Church for the last decade, I have noticed that many believers are confused about faith. So the first two sec-tions of this book will clarify a lot of misconceptions and confusion about how to exercise effective faith. As we move through this subject, we are going to assimilate many practical points about having faith. We will come to a well-rounded understanding of the different ways faith works. Then, in part 3, we will look at why faith is at times difficult. What are the enemies of faith that particularly impact us today? Are there effective, balanced answers to those difficulties? Yes! We will see what they are. And in part 4 we will explore some of the more subtle implications of having faith.

This book will set you, the reader, free to confront the challenges, subtleties and opportunities of having effective faith. It will give proper attention to the complexities of faith without diluting your ability to take faithful action. It will also, I hope, answer long-standing confusions you may have had about the theory and practice of faith.

In this first section we will take a look at the matter of faith from God's perspective. He has a stake in our faith, and we want to let His interest in it settle into our minds.

Before we get into the subject, however, let me introduce myself. I am what you might call an "anointed averagite." Nearly everything about me is average: I am 5'10" tall, weigh 164 pounds, have average looks, drive an ordinary car and live in a typical house. My four sons are pretty normal, my sins nothing spectacular, I do not command attention as I walk down the street and, except for a passion for Oriental food, what I eat is fairly standard. I sleep seven hours a night, watch 1.5 hours of TV per day, read a dozen books a year and take a three-week vacation. I pastor an average-sized congregation, dislike yardwork, have hair that is graying at the usual rate and laugh at a clever joke.

That is the average part. The anointed part is that you never know in what wonderful ways the Lord is going to break out in the worship services I lead, I have managed to get almost everybody in our church involved in some hands-on ministry, I have seen incredible healings occur under my own hands, God manages to place me in front of the right persons at the right time for the right purpose with astonishing regularity, I and my congregation exer-

cise a worldwide ministry in putting on power ministry
conferences (over 130 of them to date), and a steady
stream of reports comes in testifying to changed lives
because of our ministries and my writings.

Please do not take these comments as an inflated concept of my greatness. I have been tutored by the Lord Himself concerning the limits of my capacities and have come
to agree with His assessment completely, that I can do
nothing without Him.

Also, honesty compels me to state that I am not *always*
anointed. I do not always walk in the purposes of God, I
am not always bearing God's power and sometimes I have
feet of clay up to my navel. I do not want you to get the
idea that there is anything special about me that is not
available to any believer.

I am the average part and God is the anointed part, but
one without the other is ineffective. As long as God keeps
on deciding to do His work through people, He needs folks
like me and you. As long as I keep on realizing that I cannot do anything by myself, I have to have His help.

Well, since we cannot do anything by ourselves, this
brings us to our investigation of the subject of this book—
the business of having faith. First, let's set the frame of
reference.

The Bible speaks of four kinds of faith. It is important
to distinguish them briefly so we will not get confused
later on.

> The first is *the* faith, which is a collection of proposi-
> tions about God. The creeds, for example, are state-
> ments of the faith. Later on we will talk about the
> difference between dogma and doctrine, which are
> two kinds of expressions of the faith. For the
> moment, it is enough to say that *the* faith is what
> Christians believe and defend as the truth.

The second is *saving* faith, which is the ability God gives people to believe in Jesus as Savior and Forgiver and Lord. This is a kind of faith that comes before normal faith. It is saving faith to say, "Jesus is Lord," when one is receiving Him into one's heart.

The third kind is the *gift* of faith, which is a sort of booster shot by which we lay hold of grace that is beyond our normal grasp. We will spend a whole chapter looking at this kind of faith.

Finally, the fourth kind is the business of *having* faith, or normal faith, which is concerned with a person's day-to-day relationship with God and the world. Most of this book is about the fourth kind, normal faith; but we will need to talk about the other kinds, too.

What Faith Does for God

Now I would like to take a look at the things that having faith does for God. We are so used to thinking about what faith does for us that I want to look first at what it does for Him. It is, after all, for His glory that we exist. The things that our faith does for God are not to be thought of as limitations on His sovereignty; rather, they are His own appointed ways for us to collaborate with Him.

Faith pleases God.
Faith releases Him.
Faith fulfills Him.
Faith satisfies Him.
Faith expands His work.
Faith discloses Him.
Faith averts His judgment.

Faith Pleases Him

The first thing faith does for God is that it pleases Him. Hebrews 11:6 plainly declares, "Without faith it is impossible to please God, because anyone who comes to him must believe that he exists and that he rewards those who earnestly seek him." This is a verse we are going to encounter several times in this book. Do you hear the tone of generosity in it? It implies that God is eager to reward His people with good things. In fact, it *pleases* Him to pour out good rewards on us. What is it that permits Him to pour them out? Faith! That is why faith is essential for Him to be pleased.

We worship and follow a gracious God. Like a father whose supreme happiness is to benefit his children, God is blessed when we cooperate with His desire to bless us.

There was a time in my life when I was not able to please God because I was unable to exercise faith in a crucial

Hard Questions About Faith

When I was thinking about this book, a friend challenged me with her hard questions about faith. I have decided to insert them into the book. Some I will answer directly, some obliquely. Some maybe you should answer. They will occur in boxes like this.

area: my own acceptability. I had grown up rejecting myself for all those average things I noted above. I did not want average looks; I wanted spectacular looks. So I rejected myself because I was unspectacular. This was a basic-level concern, a concern on which all the other con-

cerns in my life rested. God accepted me, but His acceptance went for nothing because I was unable to appreci-
ate and receive His acceptance. He was, therefore, displeased—not displeased in me but displeased in my
stiff-arming of His acceptance.

So all through my youth God was at work to bring me
to the point of self-acceptance. First He gave me affirmation through other people. I began letting people see me
as I really was and, wonder of wonders, they accepted me
anyway. This made me question the basis for my self-
rejection. If they accepted me, who was I to reject me?

Second, God made me see the counterproductivity of
my rejecting myself. How could I expect much of worth
to come forth from a being whom I thought rejectable? I
wanted to do well but did not believe I could do well, so
I was trapped in a self-wrapped counterproductivity.

Third, God gave me a hunger for self-unity. I felt like a
divided person. Part of me was always at loggerheads with
other parts of me. I came to the point where I ached for
internal unity.

Fourth and most important, God began showing me
that the basis for my self-acceptance resided in Him, not
me. He started saying things like this to me: "Mike, I don't
accept you because you are acceptable; I accept you
because I am an acceptor. If I accepted you because you
were acceptable, I would stop accepting you if you
stopped being acceptable. I don't want such a fickle basis
for your acceptance. So I accept you because I'm an
acceptor. I don't change. That means you will always be
acceptable to me."

When all that sank in, I began to see a glimmer of hope
for myself. I knew that Jesus was truly acceptable. I knew
that the Bible stated that "He has made us accepted in the
Beloved" (Ephesians 1:6, NKJV). I suspected that meant
that Jesus' true, deserved acceptability is somehow
ascribed to us as a gift if we just believe in Him.

But plenty of "evidence" was still at work to contradict the possibility of my accepting myself. I could not yet separate my self from my sin, I was distressed that I kept on sinning, if I was so wonderful why didn't I make straight A's, how come people weren't going ga-ga over me. Stuff like that.

As I said, I did decide to show myself to others with more determination, and that helped me. Their seeing who I really was and accepting me anyway put a footing under me on which I could stand and begin to accept myself. But still I held out against final, total self-acceptance.

One day I suddenly realized that all the people in the world could know everything about me and accept me, but that I would still have to accept myself, or all of their acceptance would go for nothing. I started realizing that something from *me* had to occur if this issue were to be resolved satisfactorily.

Now I was getting to the core of the matter. I was coming to the brink of faith. Something was being required of me, something that the following illustration may get at. If I really stretch my legs out, I can step over a distance of five feet. If two buildings are five feet apart, I can step from one roof to the other. But if the distance is six feet, I have to jump. What I found out is that self-acceptance is a six-foot gap. To get to the other side you have to jump. It is not a terribly far jump; it is well within your capability. But you do have to jump. You have to leave the realm of evidence and reasonability and other people's acceptance and leap into another realm, a realm where you have not been before.

This jump is faith. And it pleases God no end, for it allows Him to make amazing differences in your estimate of yourself. Once I made the leap of accepting His acceptance of me, once I started saying to myself, "Mike, you are a first-rate son of the living God," then His pleasure in me went full-circle, because it was now not only offered but also received.

Self-acceptance is not the only use of our faith that pleases God, of course. Any act of faith pleases Him, for faith allows Him to display His heart toward us. God has positioned Himself *to need something from us* in order to be pleased. That something is faith, for faith sets Him free to unload the blessings in His heart upon us. As the verse says, "He rewards those who earnestly seek him."

Faith Releases Him

The second thing faith does for God is related to the first: It releases Him. Faith is the agent of cooperation between human beings and God. It is faith that allows a person to superextend his or her ability, for example, to solve personal, political, economic and racial problems. Faith is the thing that lays hold of resources beyond our natural grasp. It is the key that the Father places in our hands to insert into His locks to release His capabilities for us.

Do you remember in school when you needed a permission slip to do something out of the ordinary? That's just what faith does: It permits God to do what He wants to do.

I was leading a gathering in Buenos Aires in August 1992. My pattern is to teach and then have a ministry time. Well, during the ministry time the Lord told me that someone was there with a hearing loss. When I asked the people if this was true, it turned out that there was a woman in her early thirties with serious hearing problems. She could not pronounce words correctly because she had not ever heard what they sounded like. So I put a couple of our team members to working with her. As they interacted with her and as they had faith, there came a *plop!* sound in her ears, after which she could hear plainly. (*How* did they "have faith"? I will tell you in chapter 3.)

It was wonderful the rest of that evening watching this woman listen to how people pronounced words and then practice them on her own. She would approach someone and say, "How do you say *tomato*?" They would pronounce it for her and she would practice saying it. Sometimes they would have to repeat the word several times. I wish you could have been there to see her eyes light up with the recognition of the true sounds of words. She was like a child in a candy store. And God was like a child in a candy store watching her benefit from this new release of His power into her life. By the time she left for home, her speech was already much improved. Her faith and the team's faith released God to help her.

This is an important investment that God has in our faith. He is all-loving, all-powerful, all-caring, all-knowing, but He is also all bound up in some true sense until His people release His all-ness into the situations that need His touch. Faith is the ingredient that releases Him. So God is always, as Jesus said, looking for people who will collaborate with Him by the exercise of their faith.

Faith Fulfills Him

Because it is such a turn-on for God when we have faith, faith also fulfills Him.

When each of my sons got to about one year of age, he started trying to walk. I would set him on his wobbly legs and remove myself by about a foot from his reach. Stretching out my hands toward him, I would beckon for him to take a step toward me. When he made that step, I would swoop him up into my proud arms, laughing and rejoicing at his success, commending him effusively for his bravery. Later the boys learned to read words, ride bikes, shoot baskets, dance with girls, drive cars and get jobs.

Each step they took did something wonderful inside me: It fulfilled me.

Faith is that responding step of the child bridging the gap between himself and his Father. Does God sometimes seem distant from you? Wonderful! It means He has a new growth level for you to achieve. And when you achieve that level, He is fulfilled, completed, triumphant.

Now don't get the idea that I am saying God is utterly dependent on the exercise of our faith in order for Him to be able to act. If that were the case, *we* would be God, not He. What I am saying is that God seems to impose a limitation on Himself that requires our collaboration with Him in order for that self-limitation to be ended.

Jesus was clearly stymied, for example, by the lack of faith among the people in His hometown: "He could not do any miracles there, except lay his hands on a few sick people and heal them. And he was amazed at their lack of faith" (Mark 6:5–6). Now is it literally true that He "could not" do miracles there? I don't think so. God can do whatever He wants. But it was operationally true that He could not, because He limited Himself to working in cooperation with people's faith.

I have learned that when Jesus commanded us to ask, seek and knock, He was referring to three different modes of prayer-relationship with Him. The focus of asking is receiving; its style is petition. The focus of seeking is finding; its style is devotional prayer. The focus of knocking is the opening of God's blessings for others; its style is intercession.

In petition, God relates to us in ways that encourage us to ask with insistence. So He may seem slow in answering because He wants us to build up a head of persistent steam.

In devotional prayer, God relates to us by appearing elusive. He wants to be a treasure that we will seek until we find. What treasure is worth keeping that allows us to find it too quickly? So when we set out to seek Him, we will eventually get to the stage where He seems pretty hard to connect with. Again, the message is: Keep going!

When we persevere, He Himself is fulfilled. It fulfills Him for us to stretch up on tiptoes to lay hold of His blessings, to mature in petition and devotion. The nature of love is to seek the blessing of the beloved. Love is not fulfilled until the beloved is blessed. Faith frees God to experience that fulfillment.

Faith Satisfies Him

Satisfying God may not seem much different from pleasing and fulfilling Him, but it is an important observation about faith. Faith is our proper work. When the Israelites asked Jesus, "What must we do to do the works God requires?", He replied, "The work of God is this: to believe in the one he has sent" (John 6:28–29). In Jesus' reply, the word translated "work" is the word that describes one's occupation. Our occupation, in other words, is to believe.

Two guys were introduced one day. One of them asked, "What do you do for a living?"

"I'm a believer," the other replied.

"No, I mean, what's your job?"

"I believe."

Frustrated, the first said, "Come on, you know what I mean!"

"My occupation is to have faith. I do plumbing to make expenses."

Now that fellow knew what life was all about. By calling faith his career, he maintained an attitude that allowed the expectations in God's heart to be satisfied. He had both a short- and a long-term view of the business of believing. Our faith fulfills God's heart; it satisfies His expectations, His plans. And sometimes those plans are fairly long-term. In an instantaneous-oriented society, it is important to have a long-haul view of faith. Just as a job or career is not something one completes in a day, so faith is an ongoing process.

I think this is why Jesus often taught on the value of perseverance. By definition, one cannot "complete" perseverance very quickly. If not lengthy in time, perseverance will at least be lengthy psychologically. The persistent widow in the parable (Luke 18:1–5) may have been coming to the unjust judge for months, but I'll bet it felt like years for her on a psychological level! The persistence of the fellow who pounded on his neighbor's door at midnight probably took no more than five minutes, but it required a psychological heaving of himself to the task each time he was refused (Luke 11:5–8).

The word in Greek for "persistence" or "importunity" is *anaidia*, which means literally "unshamely." This has two senses. A person asks shamelessly because he has been forgiven and no longer has shame. He also asks shamelessly because he is past the point of social propriety. Jesus, I think, commends both senses of shamelessness. This persistence satisfies God because it overcomes all the opposition to receiving His blessings.

Often my sons ask if they can use my Acura. I am very attached to that car. I would rather they use my old Chrysler. So I may say something like, "Why don't you use the Chrysler?" There follows a bit of dialogue in which I do not always conduct myself with the greatest generosity. But they always get the Acura if they are shameless in asking. If their need is great enough—in their eyes—they get shameless enough.

Now God is not like me. He does not resist our requests because He does *not* want to grant them, but because He *does* want to grant them. It is not that He wants us to beg; He wants us to grow in persistence.

It interests me that Jesus used the figures of an *unjust* judge and a *reluctant* neighbor to teach about persistence. God is neither unjust nor reluctant, but we may sometimes feel that He is. Jesus recognized this. That is why He said, "Ask!" "Seek!" "Knock!" The sense of the Greek is, "I command you to keep on asking." That's our part.

God's part is this: "Will not God bring about justice for his chosen ones, who cry out to him day and night? Will he keep putting them off? I tell you, he will see that they get justice, and quickly" (Luke 18:7–8). This satisfies Him for it allows Him to complete His plans for us.

Faith Expands His Work

I want to use a mechanical image to describe the next point: that faith expands God's work. Piston engines, in which the piston moves back and forth, are called reciprocating engines. The piston moving back and forth creates and deploys power to get the job done. Faith is like that reciprocating engine. St. Paul said that one of God's acts is to call "things that are not as though they were" (Romans 4:17). There wasn't something; then God acted; then there was something. This is seen especially in God's creation of the world. In God's present workings with the world, He gives us the chance to co-create with Him. The "engine of faith" releases power into circumstances, and that power changes those circumstances.

Faith is a reciprocator, a thing that passes back and forth between God and man. He gives us faith and we use it, releasing His power to work. His part is to give, our part is to use, and the thing between us is faith. Remember, faith is our proper work. Our work and His work focus on His giving and our using faith.

We need to remind ourselves that the world is in excruciating need of the power of God. In the past few years many politicians at all levels of government have been interviewed about this. Most of them realize that human resources are inadequate to the needs that confront them. This opens them up to receiving prayer, for they know that unless something from the spiritual realm comes to their aid, they are fighting a losing battle.

But that is true of all of us. We are all in need of the help of God. None of us is adequate to the demands made upon us. God recognizes this. "Apart from me," Jesus said, "you can do nothing" (John 15:5). Let me ask you a question: Is *anything good* exempt from the word *nothing?* If you can do nothing without His help, just how much hope is there for you on your own? When we come to the recognition that we absolutely must have God's help, and we ask for it in faith, we allow Him to accomplish His work.

I like that image of a reciprocating engine. It gets work done: It pumps water, propels vehicles, generates power, mixes food and all kinds of needful things. Faith is our part of the engine. It is the fuel that enables it to work.

Faith Discloses Him

If God did not choose to reveal Himself to us, we would know nothing of Him. We do not possess the ability to penetrate the barrier between the human and the divine; that penetration must come from His side. God has chosen to reveal Himself to the world, but faith is the vehicle by which we lay hold of the divine self-revelation. We will have fun later in this book discovering the faculties and procedures by which we do that laying hold. For the moment it is enough to say that God reveals Himself and that faith discloses that revelation.

What is the difference between revelation and disclosure? Well, I think of it like a Christmas present: The giver gives the gift but the receiver must open it. God gives a revelation of Himself but our faith accepts, makes use of, receives and benefits from that revelation. That is, faith *discloses* Him. It is how we open His offering of Himself to us.

You know, this business of knowing and working with God is not simple. What kind of God would He be if we could figure out everything about Him quickly? Life is too complex for that, and you can bet that God, as the Author of life, is also very, very complex. In fact, his ways are, as the King James translation puts it, "past finding out" (Job 9:10; Romans 11:33). We're just never going to exhaust comprehending who He is and what He's about.

Faith is the baseball glove that catches the fly balls of His revelation of Himself to us. He speaks to us through Scripture, through nature, through people, through our own spirits and through events. Faith is the thing He has given us by which we become aware that He speaks to us and decipher what He is saying and are enabled to do our part in disclosing Him.

Faith Averts His Judgment

God is not eager to judge people. In fact, the opposite is true. He "[delights] to show mercy" (Micah 7:18), "[takes] no pleasure in the death of the wicked" (Ezekiel 33:11), does not want "anyone to perish, but everyone to come to repentance" (2 Peter 3:9), and urges, "Save yourselves from this corrupt generation" (Acts 2:40).

But He does not cram salvation down anyone's throat. When the rich young ruler went away sad at Jesus' challenge, Jesus did not run after him, tug at his sleeve and implore, "But you don't understand what you're passing up!"

When we use the faith that God gives, we activate all the complex provisions that He has made available for our redemption, salvation, justification, purification, restoration and forgiveness.

Sin must be judged. There are two choices: Either it is judged on us or it is judged on Jesus. As C. S. Lewis once observed, "In the final analysis, there are only two kinds of people, those who say to God, 'Thy will be done,' and those to whom God says, 'Thy will be done.'" If we say to God, "Thy will be done," we will accept the birth, life, death, resurrection and reign of Jesus that save us. If God has to say to us, "*Thy* will be done," He allows us to try to make our own way in making right what we have done wrong. That decision propels us outside the temporal and eternal operation of His grace.

What Faith Does For Us

Up to this point, we have been looking at the *why* of faith for God's sake. Let's take a few minutes with the *why* of faith for our sake. Then much of the rest of this book will be about the *how* of having faith.

We have seen hints already of what faith does for us. When God is pleased, released, fulfilled, disclosed and satisfied, when His work is expanded and His judgment averted, we are the ones who benefit, of course, for need (as Norman Grubb observed) is the creditor of love.

What does it mean to say that need is the creditor of love? Well, creditors are owed something, aren't they? Love is so loving that it feels indebted to meet need's need. We have long lists of needs. Love says, "I'll meet them." And faith permits Him to do it. So faith lays hold of God and of the things of God.

Here is a list of what the Gospels say faith does for us (parallels are deleted):

In Matthew:

Faith gets us our clothing	6:30
Faith conquers fear	8:26
Faith heals us	9:22, 29
Faith permits the doing of miracles	13:58

Faith conquers doubt	15:28
Faith gets us our food	16:8–10
Faith allows God to reward us	25:21

In Mark:

Faith gets our friend forgiven	2:5
Faith gets our friend healed	2:11–12
Faith gets us our sight	10:52
Faith believes in resurrection	16:14

In Luke:

Faith elicits great commendation from Jesus	7:9
Faith influences the weather	8:25
Faith removes obstacles	17:6
Faith reverses reversals	22:32

In John:

Faith connects us with Jesus	2:11; 7:31; 8:30
Faith achieves miracles that enable others to believe	11:45; 12:11
Faith comforts us	14:1
Faith enables us to exceed Jesus' accomplishments	14:12

These are great blessings. We have a lot of growing to do, of course, in order to permit the Lord to fulfill all these possibilities. But before we tackle the difficulties and obstacles in having faith, just pause a moment to look at this list: relationship with God, provision, health, blessing for others, miracles, empowerment, influence over the natural world, eternal life.

Faith is a pivotal dynamic. We need it! We need to get good at it! We need to help others do it!

How Much Faith Do We Need?

The very notion of "how much" faith betrays a misunderstanding of what faith is. Any amount of the real thing is enough. But it is easy to get confused about this. When

---

Hard Questions About Faith

Number One: How do I know, on a "grain-of-mustard-seed scale," how much faith I have?

---

the disciples asked Jesus why they could not cast a demon out of a boy, He replied, "Because you have so little faith. I tell you the truth, if you have faith as small as a mustard seed, you can say to this mountain, 'Move from here to there' and it will move. Nothing will be impossible for you" (Matthew 17:20). Palestinian mustard is a species that produces a seed so small as to be nearly invisible to the naked eye. A thimble could hold thousands of them. So Jesus was saying to the disciples that their faith was smaller than the smallest thing He could think of. In other words, they were not operating in faith at all.

There is tremendous encouragement for us in this. If we can find the real thing, the smallest amount of it will be sufficient for the most demanding job. It is not a question of "how much" but of "what." So let's turn to an exploration of what faith is and how we can utilize it successfully.

First, let me tell you about a woman I will call Amaris. When I knew her, Amaris was in her sixties. It causes me a grinning shake of my head to remember her, for she was one tough customer. She had lived a life of hard drinking, chain smoking, tough cussing, long toiling. Her face was lined with deep creases like dried-out leather from which came a voice like Lauren Bacall's with a rasp.

Amaris' salvation had come through the surprising birth of a daughter when Amaris was past fifty. This child had completely turned her life around. Well, pretty completely—she could still let loose a string of words that would file your sensitivities down to survival level! But her lifestyle had vastly improved.

Still, her hard living had taken its physical toll. She had had two cancers removed surgically and was facing a third. One day she came to my office.

"Father," she rasped, "I want you to pray for this cancer in my bowels."

She always called me *Father*, in the tradition of the Catholic and Episcopal Churches.

"Have you been to the doctor about it?" I asked.

"Now, Father, don't you get it into your head that you're going to change my mind. I'm not having any more operations!"

"Amaris, you've got a nine-year old daughter. If they can get at that cancer, you owe it to her to let them operate. I know you're sick of operations and hospitals and recoveries and all that. But you've got to let them get it out of you."

Amaris looked at me with rounded eyes as if she had just realized the true state of my mental capacities. For a moment she hung there deciding how to have mercy on this stupidity opposing her. Then her eyes went to slits as she decided that I wasn't stupid so much as obtuse.

"Father"—her voice reached out with hands and took firm hold of my neck—"you listen to me! I'm not having any more operations! You just better pray to God so that He heals this cancer, you hear?"

The battle of the wills was over; she had won hands down. So I got up and walked over to her, instructing her to place her hands on her lower stomach. Then I put my hand on hers and prayed. It was a concerned, doubtful, hopeful prayer that God would have mercy on her and heal her. As she left my office, I wondered how I was going to help the family handle her illness, if it continued.

A week or so later the phone rang. Rasp voice. But different. Gleeful. "Father, the doctor says I'm healed!"

And she was. She had gotten her faith to reach out and grab hold of the living God, setting Him free to please and satisfy and fulfill and disclose Himself in her healing. She and God got it together, and it worked.

2

What He Has Given Us to Have Faith *With*

Many people misunderstand what it is like to exercise faith. We make two common mistakes. First, we assume that faith must be a feeling. This is understandable, for sometimes we do something because we feel it is the thing to do. If it turns out well, we conclude (naturally) that faith must be a feeling.

There *are* times when faith correlates with feelings, but many times faith is flatly unemotional. There are even times when faith must act in opposition to a feeling. If we count on *feeling* "faithful," we will not exercise faith on any consistent level.

What's more, Jesus spanked the disciples verbally for having "little faith." His opinion was that their faith was under their control. It would not have been fair to chide them for something over which they had no control, would it?

Think about your emotions for a moment. Do you control them? You may be able to control the *expression* of an emotion—in a macho refusal to cry at a movie, for example—but you cannot control the *existence* of the emotion. If someone rushed into the room right now to tell you that your best friend had just died, your emotions would take off on their own whether you liked it or not. How you responded to that news would be faithful or unfaithful, but your faith would not be the feeling. That is, you could allow feelings of devastation to cause you to act out of despondence. That is not faith. Or you could express the grief honestly but refuse to allow the emotions to cause you to act out of the feelings of despair. That is faith.

The second mistake we make is assuming that faith is based intellectually. Our minds are utilized to think about faith, of course, and carry out the mandates of faith, but faith itself is not based mentally any more than it is based emotionally. The mind has a finite capacity by which to interact with reality, which is infinite. If you could believe in only what you could understand, you would be severely crippled.

Faith sometimes requires us to act in ways that are *irra*-tional and often requires us to act in ways that are *trans*-rational. We will say more about this in chapter 5. But for now I want to plant in you a challenge to the notion that intelligence is the primary reality-comprehending faculty.

I am not at all suggesting that God is somehow opposed to emotions or intellect. He is, after all, their Creator. He likes us to have good feelings and He likes our minds to be lively. But God has a function planned for each of the capacities He has placed in us. It is the function of the emotions to feel and of the mind to think, but the function of neither of these to have faith. It is important to grasp this for, as we will see in chapter 6, the devil has access to both our emotions and our minds. Great confusion and immobilization can come to those who do not realize that faith is not primarily emotional or intellectual.

Let's unpack this more.

A Little Biblical Anthropology

There is in the Western world today a current of inclusivity and holism that has some good points. Inclusivity is a movement that includes differences instead of rejecting them. Racial differences, for example, are being addressed effectively by appealing to a "gospel" of inclusivity. Holism is an attempt to realize that various factors are ecologically, or causally, related. We see this in nature. And we see the advantages of treating medical problems from a holistic viewpoint that recognizes the roles that lifestyle, diet, genetics and macrobiotics play in contributing to illness.

Unfortunately, inclusivity and holism tend to blur the distinctions between and among human faculties for the sake of internal unity. Someone might say, "My whole being has been saved by the cross of Christ, so my whole being is involved in my relationship with Him." So far so good. But: "Therefore, it takes my whole being to respond in faith to Him." Tilt! This kind of thinking ignores the distinctions in faculties that the Lord has set in place.

We begin to understand faith by considering biblical anthropology. Once we arrive at a biblical distinction between and among our various human faculties, we discover which faculty God designed for us to have faith with. The apostle Paul gave us a running start with this encouragement:

> May God himself, the God of peace, sanctify you through and through. May your whole spirit, soul and body be kept blameless at the coming of our Lord Jesus Christ. The one who calls you is faithful and he will do it.
> 1 Thessalonians 5:23–24

He notes three major faculties in this passage: spirit, soul and body. Let me propose right off the bat that different faculties in us perform different functions.

In another place Paul draws conclusions about functioning in the Body of Christ from the example of an individual human body:

> If the whole body were an eye, where would the sense of hearing be? If the whole body were an ear, where would the sense of smell be? But in fact God has arranged the parts in the body, every one of them, just as he wanted them to be.
>
> 1 Corinthians 12:17–18

Ears are meant to hear, eyes to see, stomachs to digest and so on. A stomach that tries to see is going to be a frustrated stomach!

These differences in function start with the Trinity itself:

> There are different kinds of gifts, but the same Spirit. There are different kinds of service, but the same Lord. There are different kinds of working, but the same God works all of them in all men.
>
> 1 Corinthians 12:4–6

Paul seems to be saying that the Holy Spirit is in charge of gifts, Jesus handles service and the Father oversees works. This is not to suggest that there is any competition or disunity among the Persons of the Godhead, but simply a difference in function.

Elsewhere, the Scriptures place the responsibility for creation on the Father, for salvation on the Son and for sanctification on the Spirit. While the Spirit and the pre-existent Jesus had a role in creation, the primary originator of creation was the Father. While the Father planned the salvation of mankind and the Spirit assisted Jesus constantly, it was the Son who had to exercise obedience and get nailed to the cross. While the Father and the Son sit on the throne in heaven and dispatch the Holy Spirit to the world, it is the Spirit who conducts the affairs of God in Person on earth.

Different Persons, different functions.

Similarly, different faculties in us—spirit, soul and body—perform different functions.

Now note this:

> But God hath revealed them unto us by his Spirit: for the Spirit searcheth all things, yea, the deep things of God. For what man knoweth the things of a man, save the spirit of man which is in him?
>
> 1 Corinthians 2:10–11, KJV

Paul is comparing one of the roles of the Holy Spirit in the Trinity with the role of an individual's human spirit. He goes on correlating the Holy Spirit and the human spirit:

> In the same way no one knows the thoughts of God except the Spirit of God. We have not received the spirit of the world but the Spirit who is from God, that we may understand what God has freely given us. This is what we speak, not in words taught us by human wisdom but in words taught by the Spirit, expressing spiritual truths in spiritual words. The [*soulish man*, literally] does not accept the things that come from the Spirit of God, for they are foolishness to him, and he cannot understand them, because they are spiritually discerned. The spiritual man makes judgments about all things, but he himself is not subject to any man's judgment.
>
> 1 Corinthians 2:11–15

It is not a man's mind or emotions that know his thoughts, but his spirit. What does this mean? Or how does a woman experience her spirit "knowing her thoughts"? Not so fast! We will get there eventually, but we are on the trail of the thing we have faith with. The

38 God's Reasons for Faith

danger for the moment is to conclude that there is no difference between mind and spirit because we do not know how they differ. Let's go on by going back to the beginning for a moment.

When God was setting up the rules for Adam and Eve in the Garden, He said, "Of the tree of the knowledge of good and evil you shall not eat, for *in the day* that you eat of it you shall die" (Genesis 2:17, NRSV, italics mine). After they sinned, Adam and Eve went on living, didn't they? But they were different. Their spirits had in some significant way "died," just as God had warned. They died spiritually immediately; they died physically eventually.

It was this spiritual deadness that Jesus noticed immediately about Nicodemus in John 3. His explanation was, "Unless a man is born of water and the Spirit, he cannot enter the kingdom of God. Flesh gives birth to flesh, but the Spirit gives birth to spirit" (John 3:5–6). Jesus was telling Nicodemus that his parents had given birth to him on the natural level but that it would take the Spirit of God to give birth to him on a spiritual level. Only the Holy Spirit can reverse the death that Adam and Eve loosed on mankind by their sin. As Paul put it, "As in Adam all die, so in Christ all will be made alive" (1 Corinthians 15:22). Again, it was not just physical death but spiritual death that Adam launched and that Jesus reversed.

Perhaps a graphic illustration will help make sense of what I am trying to say. The following graphic is a composite of a number of representations constructed by strongly biblical people who have experienced hands-on collaboration with the Holy Spirit—people like Watchman Nee, Dennis Bennett, Francis MacNutt and Ian Thomas. (I have referenced this spirit-soul distinction in former books.) I should caution the reader that no two-dimensional representation of a four-dimensional reality can be entirely satisfactory; and the lines between various components are wavy, even fuzzy at points. Nonetheless, I find

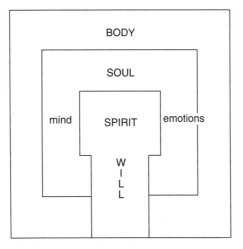

this graphic extremely helpful. I would even challenge you to memorize it. You will find it helpful.

This graphic (which we will encounter variations of several more times) represents the outermost level as the *body*. This is reasonable, for the body is that part of us most in touch with the external world. The word in Greek for body is *soma*.

The middle level is the *soul*, composed of those faculties that constitute each of us as a person: mind, will and emotions. The Greek word is *psyche*. This is what I translated above in 1 Corinthians 2:14 as the "soulish" man. The KJV translates it *natural*, the NRSV as *unspiritual*, the NIV as *without the Spirit*.

These outer two levels of body and soul are together called the *sarx*, translated as "flesh." In verse 1 of 1 Corinthians 3, Paul says, "And so, brothers and sisters, I could not speak to you as spiritual people, but rather as people of the flesh" (NRSV). As Barclay noted in his commentary on 1 Corinthians: "To Paul the *flesh* is much more than merely a physical thing. It means *human nature apart from God*, that part of man both mental and physical which provides a bridgehead for sin" (italics mine). Note that Paul was writing to Christians, calling them fleshly. One can be a believer and still choose to act out of the natural instead of the spiritual.

In the two great chapters differentiating between the flesh and the spirit—Romans 7 and 8—Paul says, "For this reason the mind that is set on the flesh is hostile to God; it does not submit to God's law—indeed it cannot, and those who are in the flesh cannot please God" (Romans 8:7–8, NRSV). So the flesh (body and soul together) does not have the capacity to please God. We must go further in toward our center before we find what it is in us that can cooperate with God, since it is apparently not our flesh.

The innermost level is the *spirit*. The Greek word is *pneuma*. It is the spirit that is reborn when we accept Jesus Christ as Savior and Lord. It is the spirit that "knoweth the things of a man." It is the spirit that is able to receive input from the Holy Spirit. It is the spirit that is able to discern spiritual things.

When you understand these three levels, you can see why Rotherham rendered 1 Corinthians 2:14 like this: "But a man of the soul doth not welcome the things of the Spirit of God, for they are foolishness unto him and he cannot get to know them because spiritually are they examined."

Barclay again comments in his book *The Letters to the Corinthians,*

> Paul speaks about interpreting spiritual things to spiritual people. He distinguishes two kinds of men. (a) There are those who are *pneumatikoi. Pneuma* is the word for Spirit; and the man who is *pneumatikos* is the man who is sensitive to the Spirit and whose life is guided by the Spirit. (b) There is the man who is *psuchikos. Psuche* in Greek is often translated soul. . . . So in verse 14 Paul speaks of the man who is *psuchikos*. He is the man who lives as if there

were nothing beyond physical life and there were no
needs other than material needs, whose values are all
physical and material. A man like that cannot understand
spiritual things.

Part of the reason the spirit is so important in understanding the things of God is that it is the part of us most

---

Hard Questions About Faith

*Number Two: How do you move to heart
faith from mere intellectual affirmation?*

---

like God Himself. God is a Spirit. We must worship Him,
Jesus said, in spirit and in truth. One who is joined to
Christ, Paul said, is one spirit with Him. When you accept
Christ as Savior and Lord, the Holy Spirit comes into your
spirit, joining Himself and your spirit in a unity that lasts
through all eternity. For God's own reasons, it is the spirit
in a person, rather than that person's mind or emotions,
that God chooses to communicate with.

Years ago the Holy Spirit gave me an analogy by which
to see these things in proper relationship to one another.
The analogy is that of a naval ship:

> The body represents the ship.
> The soul represents the lieutenants in charge of men-
> tal and emotional data.
> The spirit is the captain of the ship.
> The will is the executive officer, carrying out the com-
> mands of the captain (the spirit).

I have thought about and used this analogy for years
and it has stood the test of time. The mind and the emo-

tions provide us with important information, but neither the mind nor the emotions are meant to be in command. Rather, it is the spirit in us that is in a position of command.

The Importance of the Will

All right. Suppose I am right about this. How does one get in touch with his or her spirit? How does one's spirit (as we asked a little while ago) know his or her thoughts? How does one discern spiritual things and perceive input from the Holy Spirit? How do we know what our spirit wants us to do?

My answer, in brief, is this: by understanding the role of the will.

I know that this has been a long discussion. Maybe you are asking, "What in heaven's name does all this have to do with faith?" Just this: *The will is the faculty by which we have faith.*

Note in the graphic on page 39 that the will is represented as having an openness to the spirit that the mind and the emotions do not have. I have drawn it with no line between the will and the spirit.

There is, however, a *difference* between the will and the spirit. The spirit in us is the dwelling place of God. It is the place where we and God relate. The will in us, by contrast, is distinctly human. Somewhere there is an actual line between our spirit and our will, although no one knows where it is. That line is the site of mystery. And when it comes to the task of having faith, the spirit expresses itself in the will.

In his sermons, George MacDonald, the nineteenth-century Scottish preacher and writer, said this about the will in *Unspoken Sermons*:

> The highest in man is neither his intellect nor his imagination nor his reason; all are inferior to his will, and

indeed, in a grand way, dependent upon it. . . . For God creates in the man the power to will His will. It may cost God a suffering man can never know, to bring the man to the point at which he will will His will; but when he is brought to that point, and declares for the truth—that is, for the will of God—he becomes one with God.

Why did MacDonald say that the will is the highest faculty in man? Because it is the key to understanding and knowledge:

God forbid I should seem to despise understanding. The New Testament is full of urgings to understand. Our whole life, to be life at all, must be a growth in understanding. What I cry out upon is the misunderstanding that comes of man's endeavor to understand while not obeying. Upon obedience our energy must be spent; understanding will follow. Not anxious to know our duty, or knowing it and not doing it, how shall we understand that which only a true heart and a clean soul can ever understand?

The will, in other words, is what enables the intellect to understand. Understanding is an ability that is informed and liberated by the will. Our obedience to the promptings of God frees Him to give us understanding. It comes from our spirit through our will to our mind. As Job says, "It is the spirit in a man, the breath of the Almighty, that gives him understanding" (32:8).

Some years ago the Lord told me to reconcile with a woman in our church from whom I was alienated. We had had a disagreement about how much to charge people for weddings. She was so disturbed by my decision that she had left our church. Months later the Lord told me to go and reconcile with her. He had to tell me three times because I kept using my intellect to try to figure out in advance what would happen if I obeyed.

There is nothing ungodly about a little advance planning, but mine was an attempt at advance understanding. And I wasn't getting any! I could see all the ways it could go wrong or be used against me if I went and said, "I'm sorry." And God did not alleviate those fears. He merely kept restating His command: *Go and reconcile.*

Finally I obeyed. Only then—only then!—could I understand why it was important to reconcile with her. Only then could I experience release and unity and peace and the joy of having obeyed. At that point I had an obedience-enabled understanding of why it is important to be "doers of the word and not hearers only." I knew! Why? Because my obedience freed the Lord to impact my heart. Nothing but obedience changes our hearts like that. What's more, that woman was dead within a month from severe pneumonia. God had foreseen her death and wanted her to enter heaven in a state of reconciliation with me and others.

MacDonald again:

> He who does that which he sees, shall understand; he who is set upon understanding rather than doing, shall go on stumbling and mistaking and speaking foolishness.

In the classic devotional by Brother Lawrence, *The Practice of the Presence of God,* we read this line: "We ought to make a great difference between the acts of the *understanding* and those of the *will;* the first are comparatively of little value, and the others all" (italics mine). I disagree with Brother Lawrence's opinion of understanding—I think understanding is important—but I agree with the priority of the will.

I have discovered this sequence in the relationship between will and understanding: Exposure→Obedience→Understanding→Power. First I am exposed to some truth, usually in the Scriptures. If I obey the truth I have been exposed to, understanding follows. Understanding then opens the door to God's power. With that power I am able to collaborate with God in ways that previously were closed to me.

Some years ago, for example, I found myself taking serious note of Matthew 25:35: "I was a stranger and you invited me in." That was *exposure*. Soon after, we were presented with the opportunity to take a young street person into our home. As we considered the idea, significant reasons against taking him in rose in our thinking and in our emotions: What if he hurt our children? What if he stole from us? What if he was on drugs? As Sue and I considered these objections, we were given no proof that all would be well. What's more, our minds and emotions were unconvinced that we should do this. Nor did we understand why it was important to take him in. But we became persuaded that Jesus meant Matthew 25:35 for us.

Finally we made the decision to take him in. That was *obedience*. Only then, after he was in our home, did we gain release from fear; only then did we gain confidence that the Lord would protect us; only then were our hearts able to enfold that young man and begin to minister to his needs. That was *understanding*. The decision to trust God freed Him to prove Himself trustworthy to our minds and emotions.

But not until we acted on the decision. St. Augustine's way of putting it was like this: "Faith is to believe what we do not see, and the reward of this faith is to see what we believe."

From that point on we had *power* over fear. Whenever fear came up in our lives, we had power over it that was born of exposure, which had led to obedience, which had led to understanding, which had led to power. Obedience precedes understanding.

Questions of faith, therefore, can never be resolved on purely theoretical or theological grounds because faith insists that action be taken first. Action informs. It is the agent that releases understanding. And action is activated by the will.

It is crucial to grasp this. I have run into scores of people of intellectual integrity whose very integrity has immobilized their faith. They assume that faith is intellectual, and since they do not understand, they cannot in honesty act. Their faith is hamstrung. They sit, catch-22'd, between the demands of God that they act and their own honesty that forbids them to act. So they conclude that faith is a lot of nonsense and dismiss both its requirements and its promises.

Fitz Allison, a retired Episcopal bishop and an old seminary prof of mine, has written a book called *The Cruelty of Heresy*. While his point is about heresy, we can see in these words how he underlines the point I am making:

> Faith is not an accuracy of logic but a rectitude of the heart. The usually overlooked human factor in the origin of heresy is indeed the will that stems from the human heart. Yet authentic Christian orthodoxy is a deeper matter than mere correct doctrine, as important as that is. It must be something not less than a rectitude of heart.

What About a Weak Will?

O.K. So faith is activated by the will. But what if my will is weak? All of us have known times when our will was not strong enough to resist impulses of temptation or anxiety or anger or shame or demonization. Let's look at these in turn.

Temptation

First Corinthians 10:13 offers a very helpful promise:

> No temptation has seized you except what is common to man. And God is faithful; he will not let you be tempted

beyond what you can bear. But when you are tempted, he will also provide a way out so that you can stand up under it.

We can see two nearly opposite factors here. The first is, we are not alone in the face of temptation. Everybody gets tempted. We are not unique in this, even if we feel we are. The help that God has given to another is available to us, too.

The second, nearly opposite factor is that God has tailored the universe for us personally, individually. He will minutely monitor the influences that come your way, seeing to it that no temptation is allowed to entice you that is beyond your God-helped ability to resist. You may not care a fig for the resisting of temptation. Nonetheless, God is monitoring your temptations carefully, waiting for the day when His plans to motivate you meet with success.

Every successful resistance of temptation builds the muscle of your faith. If you have a weak will, believe that God knows precisely how weak it is and will allow nothing to come against you that you cannot resist with His aid. You may not feel confident about this ability to resist, but it will be enough.

Anxiety

Some anxiety is a conscious choice that Jesus often taught against. The middle of the Sermon on the Mount includes five parallel exhortations of "Do not worry!" (Matthew 6). The *feeling* of worry is not a conscious choice, but mental fretting is. The Bible thinks of a worrier more as a sinner than a victim, for worry is an insult to the largess and strength and wisdom of God. "Trust Me," God says to us when we are poised between turning to Him in faith and turning toward our worries in unfaith.

Some anxiety is involuntary. When this is the case, we have a responsibility to learn how to avail ourselves of God's provision for the healing of past emotional hurts that lie at the root of anxiety. Over the past thirty years, much has been learned about the ministry of inner healing. An entry-level manual, *Inner Healing*, has been written by Doug Gregg and myself.

Anger

Anger is also often the result of past emotional difficulties and can be addressed successfully with inner healing modes of prayer. Two approaches to anger are particularly good.

The first is forgiveness. When we work at forgiving others—and ourselves—we free God to root out the causes of our anger. Forgiveness dismisses the offense of the one who has hurt or sinned against us. Forgiveness puts the issue of justice in God's hands—"Vengeance is mine; I will repay, saith the Lord" (Romans 12:19, KJV)—freeing us to untangle ourselves from the fault of those who have hurt us and get on with our lives.

The second avenue in exploring anger is self-acceptance. We must let others affirm us. We must believe their affirmations. And we must make the leap of faith that our acceptance resides in a very secure place—the Lord Jesus Himself. As I noted in chapter 1, "He made us accepted in the Beloved" (Ephesians 1:6, NKJV). Jesus' acceptability, which is unchallengeable and unchangeable, is a gift to you at the moment you decide to believe in Him. It is important to affirm that truth to yourself again and again.

Shame

Shame is often a self-perpetuating dynamic that runs in a cycle beginning with a negative self-image, which leads to fear, which leads to failure, which perpetuates the negative self-image, which produces more fear, which leads to greater failure, and so on. The shamed person has been abused to the extent that it is difficult to break out of a negative self-image on his or her own. Shame is almost always victim-based in its origin, but it leads its host to become a victimizer of others if it is not checked with the healing power of God.

Demonization

An additional challenge to a weak will is demonization. The thrust of demonization is to turn one's will over more and more to the demonic being that has gained entrance to one's personage. A number of current books deal effectively with this subject, and there is a lengthy chapter on it in *Inner Healing*. Here I will say simply that even if a person has become thoroughly demonized—a rare occurrence in Christian countries—God still monitors the condition closely and will give that person the ability to willfully resist the influence of the demon.

Strengthening Your Will

If I were to ask you what you could do to strengthen your will, you would be able to provide an effective answer. It is obvious, isn't it?

Go to church, because that is where people who know God hang out.

Read the Bible, because that is the primary source of discovering what God wants us to do.

Practice doing small things only because God wants you to do them.

Love others, keep a look out for temptations, decide to believe God.

A character in a novel by Charles Williams is being hunted down by exceedingly evil people. Every time they close in on him, he responds, "This also is Thou; neither is this Thou." That is one of the most faithful statements one can make. The first phrase means: "Hmmm, well, I suppose You've allowed this to occur and that You mean to bring good out of it." The second means: "You're not limited to this, nor are You the author of it."

Later this character says in a conversation, "No one can possibly do more than decide what to believe."

Precisely.

Imagination

I need to discuss one last factor before I can close this chapter. Imagination is important because it is one way of describing the tie-in between spirit and mind. Imagination is one of the functions by which we become aware of what our spirit wants, and it is a key element in hearing God. When you hear from God, you know what He wants you to have faith for.

In former eras of church history, there have been unfortunate misunderstandings of the roles of the faculties of the soul. William DeArteaga in *Quenching the Spirit* comments on a conclusion prominent in the days of the Great Awakening:

> In all forms of faculties psychology [a Middle Ages attempt, based on Aristotle, to understand the relationship between the mind and soul] the intellect was given not only the highest status but rulership over the other areas of the mind and soul. . . . This scheme had the indirect and unintended result of placing a low value on the function of imagination, little comprehending its role in creative thinking.

Imagination involves the intuition, which seems to be a function of the spirit more than of the intellect. Let me offer an analogy by which we might comprehend the difference between mind and intuition. The human spirit is like the receiver in a TV set. It is the thing to which the signal is beamed. But the signal has to be translated in order for intelligible pictures on the screen and sounds through the speaker to occur. In this analogy, the mind is like the screen and the emotions are like the speaker. It is imagination that acts as translator from the spirit to the mind.

Let me recall a story by my friend Doug in *Inner Healing* to illustrate this point:

> I had been praying with others in a small group for Cynthia for several minutes regarding allergies, medical problems, and anxiety—especially anxiety about her health. Not much was happening, and we were preparing to close, as I asked the Lord one more time, under my breath, "Jesus, what are You doing; how are You praying for Cynthia?"
>
> Immediately I saw, in my imagination, a word in the distance, coming closer. It was a long word, beginning with the letter *m*, but I could not read it. It was like trying to read the smallest line on the eye doctor's chart. And the word wasn't getting any closer. "What is that, Lord?" I asked. And I heard the word *mendacity*. I knew I had heard that word before, but for the life of me I could not remember what it meant. Since there was a pause, I asked, "Does anyone know what the word *mendacity* means?" No one did, but Cynthia hopped up and got her dictionary and looked up the word. "It means 'the quality of being mendacious,' and that means being 'false or untrue.'"

Doug's intuition was the part of him that received the *m* and then the full word from God. It was his imagination that translated it to his mind, enabling him to begin making sense of the impression he was receiving. Cynthia, as the story continues, was believing a lie that was exposed and dealt with by the Lord, working through Doug's team.

Intuition is a valid, if mysterious, phenomenon. Most creative people have learned to allow intuition to guide their creative pursuits. Humphrey Carpenter recalls a comment by J. R. R. Tolkien about the writing of his *Lord of the Rings* trilogy:

> I met a lot of things on the way that astonished me. The Black Riders were completely unpremeditated—I remember the first one, the one that Frodo and the hobbits hide from on the road, just turned up without any forethought. . . . And then in the inn at Bree, Trotter sitting in the corner of the bar parlour was a real shock—totally unexpected—and I had no more idea who he was than had Frodo.

Trotter, later renamed Strider, ends up being a pivotal character in the trilogy.

It is the will that brokers between the intuition and the intellect, giving "permission," as it were, for the intuition to be taken seriously. The will can say to the mind, "Pay attention to this, whether you understand it at the moment or not."

When answering a friend who had written about problems with wandering thoughts in prayer, Brother Lawrence replied (italics mine):

> You tell me nothing new; you are not the only one that is troubled with wandering thoughts. Our mind is extremely roving; but, as *the will is the mistress of all our faculties*, she must recall them, and carry them to God as their last end.

In a later chapter I will look at how the intellect came into an unwarranted ascendancy in Western civilization. For the moment, let us get these points down: God has placed various faculties within us. They are all good, though they may all be used for ill. Each of these faculties is unique in the role it plays in and for us. A proper conception of our faculties, which do not have to agree with one another when it comes to matters of their peculiar domain, greatly helps in the exercise of effective faith.

Inspiration especially is a matter of intuition. The intellect does not have to comprehend the worth of an inspiration before action can be taken on the basis of the inspiration.

Thought is particularly the domain of the mind. The emotions do not have to feel positive about a given line of thought before action can be taken on the basis of those thoughts.

Feelings uniquely tap into and give expression to the emotions. The worth of a feeling need not win intellectual approval before the worth of that feeling is established.

And faith is a matter of the will. Faith is action-based, results-oriented, relationship-dependent and grace-inspired. Neither intellect nor intuition nor emotion need deter the will in the legitimate exercise of effective faith.

Now let's see how.

Part 2

The Ways
of Faith

In this second section of the
book, we want to leave some of the
background, the theoretical aspects of
faith, and look more practically at how it
works. We will define faith with more
operational emphasis and then look at a
number of effective methods for "growing
faith in our own backyard."

3
How Faith Works

In order to clarify our thinking about how faith works, it helps to have a functioning definition of what it is and what it is not. Let's begin with what faith is not.

What Faith Is Not

- First, it is not certainty. Our society places high value on research, verification and objectivity as central to the discovery of truth. These values have facilitated the benefits of the scientific method: medical knowledge, mechanical inventions and many more great things. On the day-to-day level, we want to be sure before taking action. This is surely reasonable, for none of us wants to make a mistake.

  But good old God bops along and puts the verse in the Bible that I noted in chapter 1: "Without faith it is impossible to please God" (Hebrews 11:6). If you insist on being sure, in other words, you will probably *dis*please God, because faith means taking action in the absence of certainty. If you are sure, you are probably not having faith; if you are having faith, you are probably not sure.

- Second, faith is neither a feeling nor a logical conclusion, as we saw in the last chapter.
- Third, faith is not manipulation of the divine. You cannot use faith to get God to do what He does not want to do.
- Fourth, nor is faith the price you have to pay to get something out of God. It takes faith to release God to act, but faith is not payment for His action. What you receive from God is a gift, already paid for by His own generosity.
- Fifth, faith is not a merely human phenomenon. God is involved in faith up to His hairline. He initiates, quickens, informs, enables and responds to our faith.
- Sixth, faith is not a substitute for responsibility. The Bible is loaded with things it expects us to do. In fact, faith is a *do* rather than an *is* kind of thing. You do not *have* faith so much as you *do* faith. St. Paul, for instance, said, "If a man will not work, he shall not eat" (2 Thessalonians 3:10). So it will not do to refuse to work, believing that God will place food on your table. Rather, you should faithfully work, trusting God to make your resources adequate to your need.
- Seventh, faith is not for the aggrandizement of persons. It is not to be used to enhance one's reputation or put others down or elevate one over another.

What *Is* It?

First Chronicles 5:20 claims, "He answered their prayers, because they trusted in him." If faith is what permits God

to answer our prayers, it must be important to grasp what
it is.

The clearest biblical definition of faith occurs in
Hebrews 11:1. Some translations are more helpful than
others, so let's compare a few of them. I have italicized the
two key words in each verse and given each translation a
grade:

> "Faith is being *sure* of what we hope for and *certain* of
> what we do not see" (NIV): C–

> "Faith means putting our full *confidence* in the things
> we hope for; it means being *certain* of things we can-
> not see" (Phillips): B–

> "Faith gives *substance* to our hopes, and makes us *cer-
> tain* of realities we do not see" (NEB): B

> "This *trust* in God, this faith, is the firm foundation
> under everything that makes life worth living. It's
> our *handle* on what we can't see" (TM): B

> "Faith is the *assurance* of things hoped for, the *convic-
> tion* of things not seen" (NRSV): B+

> "Faith is the *substance* of things hoped for, the *evidence*
> of things not seen" (KJV): A+

The two key words, the ones italicized in each verse
above, are important to trace back to the Greek. The first
word is *hypostasis,* meaning the real nature or reality or
essence of something. The word literally means "that
which stands under." It is the reality-base of something.
So the first phrase of the verse might go like this: "Faith
stands under the thing you are hoping for" or "Faith is the
reality-base of things hoped for."

The thrust of this phrase is that faith is real; it is substantial. Faith is not wispy, unreal, insignificant. Rather, it is essential—of the essence.

There is also a substitute quality about it. Faith stands in for what is hoped for. Faith is the essence of the thing one hopes will come. It takes the place of the thing hoped for until that thing arrives. Once it arrives, you do not need to have faith anymore.

The second word is *elegmos*, a legal term meaning proof or evidence. It is what convicts a criminal. So the translations that use the phrase *the conviction of things not seen* are on target. The substitutive sense of this phrase is that faith maintains a conviction of what you do not see until you do see it. Once you see it, you no longer need the conviction.

So faith is a present, substantial behavior that takes the place of the future, coming thing until it arrives. It is the conviction that what you do not yet see, you will see.

When I was in seminary, I loaned a number of expensive reference books to a fellow student who wanted to do a research project one summer. But when fall classes resumed, this fellow did not return to seminary, having decided to stay in Virginia. I wrote him to send me my books. No response. I know I am a bookaholic, but I really needed those books, so I wrote him again. Again, no response. About two months after I first wrote, I wrote a third time. A week later a postcard came from Railroad Express Association, telling me that a shipment from Virginia would be arriving in about two weeks. Immediately I was at peace about my books.

Someone might ask, "Why were you at peace? You still didn't have the books." I would reply, "Yes, but I had the evidence that they were coming." The postcard stood in for the books until they could be delivered to me.

That is what faith does: It stands in for what we have asked for until God can get it to us. That is the special, substitutive nature of faith. Faith actually takes the place of the thing we ask God to do until He does it.

What's more, faith releases Him to do it, as we saw in chapter 1.

How Does It Work?

Faith is an amazing gift. Let's take a bird's-eye look at it.

1. God wants to do something for us.
2. He tells us—through need or the Bible or our imagination or someone else—what it is He wants to do.
3. He gives us the faith to ask for it.
4. We willfully exercise this faith.
5. Our faith frees Him to be at work on the project. As we "do" faith, He continues preparing the answer to our request.
6. In the meantime, our faith takes the place of the answer. It takes the place of the answer toward God, freeing Him to be at work on it; and it takes the place of the answer toward ourselves, building in us a receptivity for the answer.
7. When the time is right, God sends the answer to us.

Everyone wants to know, of course, *when* we will see what we have asked for. In the case of the gallery of saints displayed on the walls of Hebrews 11, none of them saw what they were having faith for in this lifetime: "All these people were still living by faith when they died. They did not receive the things promised; they only saw them and welcomed them from a distance" (Hebrews 11:13). What the writer to the Hebrews is referencing, of course, is the coming of Christ.

Others in that chapter did receive more immediate results by their faith. Abraham, Isaac, Jacob, Joseph, Moses, Rahab and many others are commended for their faith, with particular results noted. The writer concludes with a flurry of the fruit of faith, citing the heroes

> who through faith conquered kingdoms, administered jus-
> tice, and gained what was promised; who shut the mouths
> of lions, quenched the fury of the flames, and escaped the
> edge of the sword; whose weakness was turned to strength;
> and who became powerful in battle and routed foreign
> armies. Women received back their dead, raised to life again.
>
> verses 33–35

Some things cannot be answered until the distant future, even the hereafter. Other things are for the present. But in either case faith is commended.

As we wrap up this definition of faith, let's look briefly at a final Greek word, the word for faith itself, *pistis*. It means to be persuaded. It does not mean that something must be proven. Again, faith here is not certitude. I do not have to be sure in order to obey the Lord, only persuaded that He is telling me to do something. Do you remember the story in the last chapter about when Sue and I took in a stranger? We were not *sure* we should take him in, but we became *persuaded* that we should.

Pistis also has a sense of reliance upon, not mere cre-dence. As Vine's *Expository Dictionary* puts it: "[Faith is] a firm conviction, producing a full acknowledgement of God's revelation or truth." It is "a personal surrender to him . . . [or] conduct inspired by such surrender." It is "a pledge of fidelity." Faith, then, is no impersonal concern. One has to care about the outcome of one's faith. It means putting your heart into it.

The Growing of Faith

Remember that faith is not a commodity we must go out and acquire. Romans 12:3 speaks of "the measure of faith God has given you." We may assume that God takes responsibility for making faith available to us. What's more, He also holds Himself responsible for the opportunity for our faith to develop.

C. S. Lewis wrote in his essay "The Efficacy of Prayer" that he once heard an experienced Christian observe:

> I have seen many striking answers to prayer and more than one that I thought miraculous. But they usually come at the beginning: before conversion, or soon after it. As the Christian life proceeds, they tend to be rarer. The refusals, too, are not only more frequent; they become more unmistakable, more emphatic.

Is this true? Yes, I think it is. Then what is the issue here? Is God a sadist?

After pondering this pattern for a while, I remember that faith is like a muscle. Muscles grow and remain strong only by being *resisted.*

A friend was bedridden for several months recently with a severe illness. When he became well enough to get out of bed, his thighs were about half their original size. They had atrophied and were terribly weak. This friend's doctors have put him on a careful regimen of diet and exercise in order to build up his muscle power. But it will take months for him to regain his full strength.

The point is, our God minutely monitors the circumstances of our lives in order to provide just the right amount of challenge to help our faith continue to grow. The muscle analogy helps us understand that none of us becomes a giant of faith overnight. The growth of our faith is a carefully engineered process. God will not let us be faced with challenges beyond our ability to meet, nor is He likely to allow many challenges to come our way that we could easily surmount.

Challenged Faith

There is a remarkable example of God's testing—strengthening—of faith in the story of the Syrophoenician woman in Matthew 15:22–28. The testing took the form of four rebuffs.

The first rebuff:

> A Canaanite woman from that vicinity came to him, crying out, "Lord, Son of David, have mercy on me! My daughter is suffering terribly from demon-possession." Jesus did not answer a word.

The second rebuff:

> So his disciples came to him and urged him, "Send her away, for she keeps crying out after us."

The third rebuff:

> He answered, "I was sent only to the lost sheep of Israel." The woman came and knelt before him. "Lord, help me!" she said.

The fourth rebuff:

> He replied, "It is not right to take the children's bread and toss it to their dogs."

This lady just kept coming back! She refused to give up. Every time Jesus or His disciples rebuffed her, she pressed back with another attack against their seeming reluctance to help her. And each time, something in her faith must have been strengthened. Finally she broke through to the level of faith that would allow God to do for her what she needed:

> "Yes, Lord," she said, "but even the dogs eat the crumbs that fall from their masters' table." Then Jesus answered,

"Woman, you have great faith! Your request is granted."
And her daughter was healed from that very hour.

The first rebuff was silence. Can you identify with her?
Have you ever felt that God was turning a deaf ear to your
request? Her response was to lean on His friends. "Make
Him help me!" she probably said.

The second rebuff was an attempt by those very friends
to dismiss her. Have you ever felt that the church was trying to dismiss you? That it would be just as glad if you went
away?

The third rebuff was a statement ("I was sent only to
the lost sheep of Israel") that disqualified her from Jesus'
attention. Her response: a simple restatement of her need.

The fourth rebuff was a racial slur—from Jesus Christ,
yet! Have you ever had the feeling that God preferred some
other class of humanity to yours? Her response was to
accept the slur, humble herself, yet find a way to use the
slur for her need.

Jesus called this "great faith." Silence, an unsympathetic
church, disqualification from His attention, even comments with racial overtones—these do not look positive,
do they? Yet these negative factors were orchestrated carefully by a loving Savior to bring His child to the point
where He could meet her need.

Think of how she might have responded to the rebuffs.
To silence she could easily have turned aside, assuming
that somehow she was defective. To His unsympathetic
friends, she could easily have reacted with disappointment
and a stinging rejoinder. To her apparent disqualification
she could have chosen to slink away amid feelings of rejection. And to the racial slur she might have made a rude
remark and stalked away in righteous indignation.

Now hear me: I am not recommending these rebuffs
toward the needy! I *am* recommending the woman's attitudes and responses to the rebuffs, trusting that some-

how, in some way, our need will be met if we persevere. Do not take God's role; take the woman's role. God may not cause some of the rebuffs we face, but He can use anything if we persevere, meeting each challenge with renewed determination.

James says this right after the opening salutation in his letter:

> Consider it pure joy, my brothers, whenever you face trials of many kinds, because you know that the testing of your faith develops perseverance. Perseverance must finish its work so that you may be mature and complete, not lacking anything.
>
> verses 2–4

What an attitude! Be joyful when you are being tested? That's faith!

Burdened Faith and Resting Faith

John 4 tells another story that is helpful in revealing a pattern of two stages of faith. A royal official in the town of Capernaum had a son at the point of death. When he heard that Jesus was in the region, he went up to Cana, where Jesus was, and "begged him to come and heal his son" (verse 47).

At first Jesus dealt with this official much as with the Canaanite woman: "Unless you people see miraculous signs and wonders, you will never believe" (verse 48). Doesn't look too eager, does He? In fact, He looks downright uncooperative and sounds a little judgmental.

But then:

> The royal official said, "Sir, come down before my child dies." Jesus replied, "You may go. Your son will live."
>
> verses 49–50

How come this guy had to overcome only one rebuff? *I don't know.* Maybe he couldn't take more than one. Maybe his faith was already almost where it needed to be and one rebuff got it over the top. In any event, it was right for him.

Notice that Jesus did not do exactly as the official requested. He wanted Jesus to go back home with him to Capernaum, and Jesus did not do that. He just said, "You may go. Your son will live." Hmmm. Put yourself in the official's place. Do you accept Jesus' mere word for it, or do you keep trying to get Him to come with you?

> The man believed the word that Jesus spoke to him and started on his way.
>
> verse 50, NRSV

You could not travel the roads at night in those days, so he had to wait till the next day to finish his journey home. En route he meets his servants who tell him his child is alive. When they compare notes, he realizes that the boy began to recover at the very time Jesus had said, "Your son will live." Now look at the official's response:

> So he himself believed, along with his whole household.
>
> verse 53, NRSV

Wait a minute! I thought he *already* believed, when Jesus spoke the word to him back in verse 50.

He did. But there is *burdened faith* and there is *resting faith*; there is anxious faith and there is answered faith. When God speaks a word to you and you seize it, you do not know what the outcome of the matter will be. You believe, but it is a burdened belief. It has an edge to it. You have fears yet to deal with. Doubts assail you, and you can easily envision how the desired answer may not come.

But if you act on the word that has been given to you—if, as the NIV puts it, you take Jesus at His word and go your way—you free God to act to fulfill the word He has given you. When the answer comes, your burden flies away. Now you believe with a different quality of faith. It is resting faith now, answered faith. It is a joyful, "I-can't-believe-it's-true," exultant faith. It is amazed, peaceful, celebratory. It is the kind of faith that makes us say, "Why can't it *always* be like this?"

Note that this quality of faith is catching. Not only the official but also "his whole household" believed. This is evangelistic faith—an exponential explosion of faith that is released in the hearts of many who observe a demonstration of the Spirit's power. In the book of Acts two whole communities came to saving faith in Jesus when the Holy Spirit healed a paralytic through Peter's prayers: "All those who lived in Lydda and Sharon saw him and turned to the Lord" (Acts 9:35).

In chapter 1, I mentioned the restoration in Buenos Aires of a woman's hearing that occurred in August 1992. During that same visit, a nine-year-old girl was healed of a congenital kidney disorder. Over the next few days her mother, father, grandmother, aunt and her parents' friends all came to faith in Jesus with an ease that surprised them. Her healing enabled them to catch that resting quality kind of faith.

Word-Quickened Faith

Another way faith is grown is for it to be quickened, or brought forth, by the Bible. The Scripture itself testifies about the Word that it is alive and sharp, it is like a hammer that can break a rock into pieces, it is like the rain that produces crops. There is an interesting thing about the word *word* in the Greek. Two very different words are both translated *word*. The first is *logos*. The sense of *logos* is that of the universal or general Word of God. The second is *rhema,* which has a narrow, particularized sense. When God quickens a part of the *logos* to be applied specifically to a situation in your life, it becomes a *rhema*—a partic-

---

Hard Questions About Faith

Number Three: How is hearing the Word of God supposed to develop my faith?

---

ular word for a particular reason aiming toward a particular outcome.

Many, many Christians have had the experience as they are reading along in Scripture of having a word or a passage jump out at them. At other times a verse from the Bible may come to mind. In such cases the Lord may be giving them a rhema, a portion of the Word that He wishes them to act on or take encouragement from.

A rhema may not mean what it means in the context of the passage from which it comes. I was on a weeklong prayer retreat once at a campsite in the high desert. After four days I was terribly lonely and realized I was not mature enough for a full weeklong retreat. So I asked the Lord if I could go home.

Psalm 34:7 flashed through my mind.

I picked up my Bible and read, "The angel of the LORD encamps around those who fear him, and he delivers them."

The word that got my attention was *encamps.* I realized—though someone might have said I was crazy or taking the word out of context—that the Lord was telling me He wanted me to stay in camp and stick it out. Reluctantly I decided to stay.

The result? Over the next three days the Lord gave me a clear vision for my ministry that lasted for the next several years. So it was worth it. But the passage in its context means nothing like *Stay in camp.*

You see what I mean?

When Paul wrote, "Faith comes by hearing, and hearing by the word of God" (Romans 10:17, NKJV), he used the word *rhema.* In other words, the Word of God must be particularized for the hearer in order for it to bring the hearer to faith. Paul also used the word *rhema* when he spoke of the weapon of "the sword of the Spirit, which is the word of God" (Ephesians 6:17). That is, a particular word spoken to the enemy in a particular situation will have the effect of attacking his influence.

How do you know that the portion of God's Word you are trying to particularize is from the Holy Spirit? First, it will concur with the general thrust of Scripture. The Spirit will not tell you to steal in order to benefit His Kingdom, because the Scriptures clearly state, Do not steal. The more we saturate our minds with Scripture, the easier it is to detect a thought or impression that is not from God. Second, the Word that comes to mind will probably challenge you somewhat. It may engender a bit of fear as you contemplate acting on it. Third, even though it may stretch you, you will have peace about it in the center of your being. This is the peace that passes understanding: "I don't know how this will turn out, but I have peace to proceed anyway." I tend to experience that peace in the region of my breastbone. It works as stillness. *Un*peace works as agitation and says *no.*

When God quickens your faith through the Bible, you can willfully lay claim to the answer.

Persevering Prayer

Throughout this book we will run into the idea of perseverance. Here is another instance of persevering as it relates to having faith.

For a time I kept a prayer journal in which I recorded prayer requests. When the answers came, I wrote them down, noting the dates. It was faith-building to keep that journal! On one occasion I wrote a prayer request about my wife, in whom there was something I wanted God to change. I prayed persistently. But as I prayed I began to see something. A couple of weeks later I had to scratch out the prayer request and enter a modified version, for I realized that the prayer in its original form was unanswerable. Then, a week later, I had to scratch out the second version—which now I also saw as unanswerable—and enter a third. Do you know what? It was not until I got to the fourth version that the prayer was answerable. I had to pray that version only a couple of days before God answered it.

This is one of the reasons, I am sure, that Jesus commanded us to keep on asking, keep on seeking, keep on knocking. When you are praying a prayer that God does not want to answer, you are nonetheless in contact with Him. That contact allows Him to change your thinking and modify the prayer, bringing it into a form that agrees with His will.

Do you have any prayers that seem to defy answers? You might take each prayer to the Lord and say, "Do You want me to change this prayer?"

God-Built Faith

Another way faith is grown can be learned from the story of Lazarus in John 11. You remember that things had gotten pretty hot for Jesus in Jerusalem, so He retired with His band across the Jordan River. There He received a message that Lazarus was sick. The first thing Jesus said was, "This sickness will not end in death" (verse 4).

Now, remember that. And remember who said it. Jesus Christ, the Son of the living and almighty God and sovereign Lord of the universe, stated, "This sickness will not end in death."

Then in verse 11 He said, "Our friend Lazarus has fallen asleep; but I am going there to wake him up." Why did Jesus say that? I think because faith looks ahead to the result of faith. In Jesus' mind He was going to Bethany to interact with Lazarus in such a way that it would have been *as though* he had been asleep. Well, the disciples forced Jesus to say, "Lazarus is dead." But He continued, and mark this: "For your sake I am glad I was not there, *so that you may believe*" (verse 15, italics mine). That was the point of the whole episode: that they may believe.

But didn't Jesus say Lazarus would not die? Not quite. He said, "This sickness will not *end* in death."

Next, Lazarus' sister Martha received the challenge to believe: "I am the resurrection and the life. He who believes in me will live, even though he dies; and whoever lives and believes in me will never die. Do you believe this?" (verses 25–26). As soon as she answered, "Yes, Lord," He went on to the next item on the agenda, for belief was His agenda for Martha.

Later He was standing outside the tomb. His question to Martha was: "Did I not tell you that if you believed, you would see the glory of God?" (verse 40). There it is again, belief! Jesus stated in the face of the cold, hard fact of Lazarus' unbreathing body, "Did I not tell you?"

Then He prayed aloud so that all could hear. Once again the focus of His prayer was belief: "Father, I thank you that you have heard me. I knew that you always hear me, but I said this for the benefit of the people standing here, *that they may believe* that you sent me" (verses 41–42, italics mine).

What was the result of the raising of Lazarus? "Many of the Jews who had come to visit Mary, and had seen what Jesus did, put their faith in him" (verse 45).

The entire episode was a setup by God from beginning to end to serve this goal: "So that you may believe." And it worked. The disciples believed. Martha believed. The Jews believed.

God wants us to believe far more than we want us to believe. He is intensely interested in building our faith.

If God's part is to build our faith, what is *our* part? Our part is to listen to what He says, hang onto what He says, refuse to let the "facts" take the place of what He says and wait for Him to make good on what He says. That is why I stress that faith centers in the will. It takes the will to overcome the attack of the facts on the intellect and emotions.

To repeat, God wants us to believe far more than we want us to believe. He is intensely interested in building our faith.

Faith Understands Authority

There are only two people whom Jesus declared had great faith. The first is the Syrophoenician woman we already looked at in this chapter. The second was a Roman centurion who asked Jesus to heal his sick servant. When Jesus agreed to go to his house, the centurion gave this reply:

> Lord, I do not deserve to have you come under my roof. But just say the word, and my servant will be healed. For I myself am a man under authority, with soldiers under me. I tell this one, "Go," and he goes; and that one, "Come," and he comes. I say to my servant, "Do this," and he does it.
>
> Matthew 8:8–9

The centurion had observed Jesus at work and realized that He had authority from God. And Jesus' reaction to his comment? "I tell you the truth," He exclaimed, "I have not found anyone in Israel with such great faith" (verse 10).

Do you know the difference between power and authority? Power is might, authority is right. Someone with a gun can force you to do what he wants because he has power over you. But someone with a uniform can get you to do what he wants because he has authority over you. I dare say most of us realize that God has power, but I suspect we poorly understand the authority given to us to release that power. Jesus had both power (from the Holy Spirit) and authority (from his relationship with the Father).

Authority comes from two sources. First, it comes from our growing awareness of and belief in who Jesus is. We must keep pondering who He is and what He did and what He yet does. Authority also comes from our growing awareness of who we are in Christ Jesus, of what His commissions to us mean and of the principles and procedures by which we step out in obedience to His commands.

Summary

Faith, then, is the agent of incarnality. It is that faculty in us that allows God to demonstrate His Word in the world. Jesus revealed the Father to the world in fleshly form. We also demonstrate His love and power today. The dynamic that frees His love and power from the realm of the potential to the realm of the actual is faith.

In the next chapter we will look at very practical methods by which to "do" faith and demonstrate Jesus' love and power.

4
Effective Methods and Models

It is important for me to begin this chapter by restating that God is the one who "agendizes" our faith. He is more interested than we are in our having effective faith, because the more effective we are at the business of having faith, the more influence He has in the affairs of humankind.

While it is God who agendizes our faith, it is our role to engage in various exercises through which we can experience and grow in faith. This chapter sets out more than a dozen methods that I have found effective.

But first let's deal with negative faith.

Exposing Negative Faith

Everybody has faith. Faith is a given. The question is not whether we are exercising faith, but what kind of faith we are exercising. There is strong faith and weak faith, effective faith and ineffective faith, positive faith and negative faith.

Negative faith is belief in what is negative. If I persist in the belief that something negative will occur, the prospects of its happening actually increase. This is one of the reasons the Scriptures often repeat the injunction "Fear not!" Fear can release negative faith. When Jesus told the parable of the sower, He was making this point: "Consider carefully what you hear" (Mark 4:24). If our hearts are formed of good soil, the Word of God will lodge there, be received, germinate and produce a harvest. But our hearts can also be soil for the word of Satan. We will look at this in considerable depth in chapter 6. For now let me just point out that when Satan speaks a word to us, he means for it to take up residence in us and produce his crop.

I have learned something fascinating in the past few years about illness. Often when I wake up in the morning with a symptom of some illness, such as a sore throat, a thought is in my mind: *I'm getting sick.* I have come to recognize the symptom and the thought as a seed from Satan looking for receptivity in my heart. If I agree with it, guess what? I get sick. But if I reject the symptom and the thought, I tend not to get sick. How do I reject it? I just say, "I rebuke this symptom and the thought in my mind that I'm going to get sick. You symptom and you thought, beat it!" It is amazing how few illnesses I get.

Negative faith is the opposite. I once buried a young woman who was desperately afraid of the word *death.* Every time Norma heard the word she would shake her head and shriek, "Don't say that!" Somehow she had become so frightened of death that she effectively drew it to herself. She allowed her fear of death—her negative faith in death—to affect her will to the degree that she acted as though she was soon going to die. And in her mid-thirties she did.

Psychologists call this "self-fulfilling prophecy." They are aware from their clients that a person can be so mesmerized by something that, in a sense, they make it happen.

This is not magic; it is faith. Faith releases the sovereign to act upon our lives. If the sovereign is God, He works in our lives for benefit. If the sovereign is Satan, he works in our lives for misfortune. Satan is not, of course, as strong as God. But God, by giving us free will, has poised us between Himself and Satan; whichever of them has our attention is the one we are freeing to act.

Please do not take this to mean that every negative thing that happens is an indictment of wrong faith. There are other reasons for the existence of bad things. Spiritual warfare, for example, can account for negative things due to curses, temptations, accusations, harassments and deceptions from the enemy. Negative things are often a challenge to the good faith we have set ourselves to exercise.

Also, do not think that God will let Satan win for very long. I was sitting with the woman I mentioned above when she died. The doctors said she should have died several days before, but every time death approached, she shrank from it in her tremendous fear. Finally, at about two o'clock on this particular morning, I said to her, "Norma, the next time you come to that line, *look over it* and see who's there!"

About half an hour later, she physically shrank back again, staring ahead in great fear.

"Look up!" I commanded her.

She did, and her whole face changed. Her body relaxed and peace seemed to descend on her. She had finally seen Jesus and realized that He would turn death into a doorway for her to be at rest in Him.

She died peacefully just minutes later. Satan's victory was over, squashed in the onset of Norma's resurrected and eternal life.

Fear is the primary indicator that Satan is inviting us to exercise negative faith. If I allow the fear of sickness to mesmerize me, I am making a willful choice to permit sickness to approach me. If I allow the fear of poverty to captivate me, I am giving the forces of Satan permission to influence some of the factors that determine my fiscal well-being. If I permit the fear of failure to magnetize me, I set the forces of evil free to work for my failure. That is why worry, from a scriptural viewpoint, is sin. Worry rejects the care-filled statements of God to us. Worry declares that God is neither trustworthy nor strong. Worry says that its god is not God but someone or something else.

"I can't help it if I'm afraid," someone might complain. In a temporary sense this is true. We are not, as I said in chapter 2, in direct, manipulable control of our emotions. But we are in direct, manipulable control of our wills. The proper response to something fearsome is to refuse to allow it to dictate our behavior. *Feel* fear, yes, but *act* afraid, no! Negative faith is when we allow feelings of fear to propel us into actions of fear. God counsels, "Don't do it! I can get you through this. Tell the fear to buzz off. Decide to trust Me." And you know what? If you act in faith, the emotion of fear will leave, often quite soon.

What are *you* afraid of? Sickness, poverty, divorce, failure, accidents, rejection, spiders, heights, alcoholism, murder, crime, job loss? Are you afraid for your loved ones? Do you fear that bad things may happen to them?

I do not ask these questions as an indictment. Heaven knows, I have often caved in to these very fears. But God is good. Gradually He has shown me that He is stronger than anything else in all the world. Tell God you are sorry for trusting in evil and that you intend to grow stronger in trusting in Him for good.

Thanking

Merlin Carothers wrote books a couple of decades ago encouraging us to take at face value verses like Ephesians 5:20: "Always giving thanks to God the Father for everything, in the name of our Lord Jesus Christ." He pointed out that normally we translate that to mean all *good* things, while the text simply says *everything*, good and bad.

What? Thank God for bad things? Never!

Well, wait a minute. St. Paul is not saying that God is the author of bad things, just sovereign over them. Paul is saying that "all things work together for good for those who love God, who are called according to his purpose" (Romans 8:28, NRSV); that we can, therefore, trust God to work on anything; and that an effective way to trust Him is to thank Him. "Thank You, Lord" is a kind of shorthand for the following points:

1. God is sovereign, in charge.
2. God can allow even the devil to be at work because He can more than undo anything the devil does.
3. Faith is what frees God to work.
4. All things do work for good to those who love God and are called according to His purpose, part of which is to trust Him.
5. Saying *thank You* is an activity that is part of faithful behavior.
6. One does not *feel* thankful for bad things; that would be masochism. One merely, willfully, thanks God for them, thereby releasing Him to work in the circumstances.

I decided to try this thanking stuff out on a couple of bads in my life twenty years ago. Perhaps my worst bad was depression. Depression could dominate me for days and weeks at a time.

One day about mid-morning I realized I was depressed. The signs were

- I felt blah, as though my insides were covered in lead.
- All my thoughts about myself were negative.
- I just wanted to retreat into sleep.

I continued to be more depressed as the day wore on. Finally, about four in the afternoon, I was certifiable.

"Help!" I cried feebly to God.

The thought came to thank Him for the depression. I had no energy to do that, but roused myself enough to give it a feeble try. "Thank You, Lord, that I'm depressed."

No change. Several minutes of mental blah.

Roused myself again. "Thank You, God, that I'm depressed."

My mind zoned out again on the blahs.

Roused myself once more. "Thank You that I feel blah, that all my thoughts are negative, that I just want to sleep."

That monumental effort sent me into several more moments of inactivity.

But over the next few minutes I gained strength. Each time I said, "Thank You," it was as though I had more energy for the next *thank You.* Finally I set my determination to do this for the foreseeable future, which was about fifteen minutes. I thanked God for everything about the depression I could think of. Then I repeated myself. Then again.

The outcome was that 27 minutes after I began thanking Him, I found that my depression had evaporated. Honestly! It flat was not there anymore.

I was astonished, delighted, full of joy. It was that resting faith all over again. It was wonderful. For the first time in my adulthood I was in the driver's seat concerning depression. I almost could not wait for it to rear its ugly head again.

Sure enough, a few months later it came back. It was still hard to do, but I began blasting away at depression like a guerrilla soldier turkey-shooting an exposed and vulnerable target. The bullets were those two words *thank You.* Ten minutes later all vestiges of depression had vanished.

That was in November 1972. I have not had more than fifteen minutes of involuntary depression since. (On two occasions I had several days of *voluntary* depression when I was in a snit with God, but they ended as soon as I trusted Him again.)

Maybe it's just a fluke, I thought. *Or maybe it works only on me.*

But a few weeks later I had the opportunity to thank God for something relating to others.

I had pastored my church for two and a half years. Some members of the congregation—which had been suffering a major division for two decades—did not like me and had tried to get the bishop to remove me. One day I made a big mistake, which gave them more than enough ammunition to complain about me. I thought bitterly that my goose was cooked. But it came to mind to thank God for the mess I was in.

Thank God?! I reacted angrily.

But I had nothing else in my corner, so I began to thank God for the mistake I had made, for the congregation's reaction to it, for their hostility to me, for the mess I was in.

An hour later a member of the congregation came to my office. He looked different somehow than he usually did.

"Father, can we talk?" he asked meekly.

"Uh, sure," I replied guardedly, hopefully.

"Father, a bunch of us gathered at my house today to complain about you. We were really getting into it, too. But about a half hour ago I suddenly realized this was wrong. I almost got sick. I made an excuse that I needed some groceries and left. But I found myself coming here. Those are my lifelong friends, Father, and I don't want to lose them, but I can't continue to be an enemy to you. What shall I do?"

The ensuing chat began the healing of the rift that had dwelt in that congregation for twenty years. God had been looking for an opportunity to heal it. He did not make me make the mistake, but He seized on it as the opening He had been looking for. My agreeing to thank Him freed Him to work on that man and on me (in that very hour!) so that I was ready to talk to him when he came.

By the time I left that congregation nine years later, there remained not one vestige of the division that had dominated the fellowship for two decades.

Rules for thanking:

1. Don't try to con God that you *feel* thankful.
2. Tell Him you know He can turn this problem into something good.
3. Thank Him for it.
4. Thank Him some more.
5. Keep willfully thanking Him until some difference occurs.

A challenge: Why not try thanking God for everything, good and bad, for one week? Suspend evaluating the experiment until it is over. Then, at the end of the week, evaluate.

Acting As If

Faith, you recall, is a *do* sort of thing—a verb, not a noun. One of the ways to do faith is to *act as if* something were already true.

Now, you cannot act as if just any old thing were true, but things that conform to the will and guidance of God. When God spoke to Abram in Haran, Abram had to act as if the directions he had been given were actually from God. It was necessary to act as if God was going to back up what Abram thought God had said to him. This was a life-changing event in his life.

It may be that God will direct us in some life-changing way, too, but the probability is that such guidance will come after years of learning to listen.

You can "act as if" sooner than that. God's Word says, for example, that "if we confess our sins, he is faithful and just and will forgive us our sins and purify us from all unrighteousness" (1 John 1:9). So one of the things you can do immediately is act as if you have been totally forgiven. What kind of attitude would that enable you to have? What kind of regard for yourself would that permit? How would that free you to deal with guilty thoughts about past events? Someone once observed that "feelings follow faith." George MacDonald put it this way: "When will once begins to aspire, it will soon find that *action must precede feeling*, that the man may know the foundation itself of feeling" (italics mine). That is, obedient action is the basis on which the feelings to back it up may occur. Action first, feeling later.

How about extending forgiveness toward others? You can act as if you have completely forgiven another for the harm he or she has done you. Translated into behavior, this means that every time the offense comes to mind, you will meet it with the assertion that "I've forgiven that and won't dwell on it negatively anymore." It means you will refuse to get back at that person. It means you will extend unconditional warm regard toward him or her.

The experience of thousands of Christians all over the world is that when they did this sufficiently, the feelings of forgiveness eventually came.

A woman approached me at a conference I was leading. She apologized for a wrong she had done to me several years before. For several minutes I could not remember the incident she was speaking of. In fact, it was getting embarrassing because she thought she meant so little to me that I had not even been offended by her act. But I simply could not recall the event. Suddenly I realized what had happened: My forgiveness of her had caused me to forget the whole matter. Acting as if her guilt had been dismissed had freed my hurt—and the memory of it—to go away as well.

Waiting

In our busy society, waiting can be mistaken for inactivity. But waiting for God to take action is not twiddling one's thumbs wasting time. It is a peculiar quality of attention to the One who is the lead actor and a recognition of ourselves as the observer in that circumstance.

Waiting as a spiritual activity is better described by the term *waiting on*. While my son Jason waits for a better job to come along, he is a waiter in a very good restaurant. I got to watch him work one evening. Jason waits on the people sitting at the tables in his section. He is observant to meet their needs. He has learned the knack of timing, knowing when they might need his attention. He is attentive to their wishes.

Waiting on God is similar. Most of the things we ask God for require answers that come in stages. Having made our requests to God, we can decide that they are on deposit with Him. We can wait on Him with reference to our requests, noticing if He needs us to take some action. You might, for instance, be praying for someone's salvation. From time to time God might signal you to do something for the person you are praying for—some act of kindness, a note, some time spent in intercession, a word of encouragement, an invitation to an investigative Bible study. This waiting on God may be crucial to His answer to your prayers.

Waiting means having the determination to insist that God has heard you and is responding appropriately to your request. It means trusting that He will not make you wait too long. It means giving Him space in which to be working. It means trusting that He knows the best *when* and the best *what.* The farmer who digs up the seeds every week to see how his crop is doing will have a poor harvest. He must believe that the seeds are germinating nicely, even though he cannot see anything yet.

Listening

When Jesus divulged His method of working, He stated flatly, "The Son can do nothing by himself; he can do only what he sees his Father doing" (John 5:19). The sinless, healthy, brilliant Son of God claimed He could do nothing but what the Father enabled Him to do. And likewise He said of us, "Apart from me you can do nothing" (15:5). A straightforward response to these statements means that we absolutely must take seriously the business of listening to God.

Each book I have written gives detailed instructions on listening to God. My purpose in mentioning it here is much more simple. What I am after at the moment is an attitude rather than a skill. Are you aware that you *need* to hear from God? If you trust in your own wisdom or education or experience or creativity or ability to land on your feet, then you are not yet convinced of your need to hear God. But if you have had enough of you and your own abilities, then I encourage you to listen to Him—and, more, to do what He tells you.

It is not hard to hear God. Try this:

1. Sit down.
2. Think of a problem you are facing.
3. Tell God about it, and tell Him you are putting it in His lap.
4. Be quiet. Relax. Don't pray. Take at least fifteen minutes for this.
5. Lightly pay attention to the thoughts that come to you.
6. Quickly evaluate those thoughts against what you know in Scripture.
7. Do what God is telling you.

Remember the story I told earlier about apologizing to a woman I had offended? It was not hard to hear God tell me to do that. In fact, for a good while I tried hard *not* to hear it! The hard part was doing what I had been told.

Frankly, it is easy to hear from God. But I will offer this bit of advice: Do not trust in your ability to hear God; trust in His ability to speak to you. If you trust in your ability to hear Him, you are focusing on the wrong thing—yourself. But if you trust in His ability to speak to you, you are focusing where you should—on Him. He knows everything about you—your entire history, your genetic structure, the books you have read, the experiences you have had, your hopes and dreams and fears—so He knows exactly how to speak to you. Trust in that.

One other piece of advice: Do not try to attain absolute certainty that God has, in fact, spoken to you. Remember, the demand for certainty displaces faith. If you are honest with yourself, and if you realize that He speaks softly—that is, underneath the requirements of certainty—you will pretty much know when God has spoken. If you decide to follow through on what He may be telling you, you will never be far from His will. Do you know why? Well, look at it from His point of view. If He knows that you are honestly trying to obey Him, He will enter into your obedient behavior *even if it is wrong* and He will make it turn out for good.

I usually take teams of people with me when I do conferences. Once in a Southern city, one of my team members, Larry, tried to help a woman who reacted strenuously and badly to what he was trying to do. He felt as though he had made a terrible mistake. And for the next two sessions she told him he had made a big mistake. But the next day the woman came to him and said, "I know you made a mistake with me. But I've been thinking about it and have decided that God permitted you to do it because it was the best way to get me to face something in my life. Well, I faced it this morning, and God has healed me of it!" Because Larry's heart was right, God made his mistake turn out for the woman's good and for his good.

We have healing teams that work every Sunday at St. Jude's. Some on those teams have greater skill and experience than others, but I tell them all, "If people come away from you feeling loved, Jesus said that's the best that can happen."

What is Jesus telling *you* to do? As the Nike ad exhorts, "Just do it!" Jesus will cover your backside. Faith is:

1. Doing what He tells you.
2. Believing that He will make it all turn out right.

Speaking

Some foolishness has been propagated in the name of the creative power of words. We will look at this practice in some depth in chapter 7. For the moment let's look at just two Scripture passages.

Romans 4:17 says that God "calls things that are not as though they were." Here is an instance of God "acting as if." He acts as if a change is going to occur by uttering a creative word about it. God can do this effectively because He is, after all, God.

But Jesus taught in Mark 11:22–24 about our speaking powerfully:

> "Have faith in God," Jesus answered. "I tell you the truth, if anyone says to this mountain, 'Go, throw yourself into the sea,' and does not doubt in his heart but believes that what he says will happen, it will be done for him. Therefore I tell you, whatever you ask for in prayer, believe that you have received it, and it will be yours."

What this means is that a creative force is loosed when we speak out what we believe God is saying. Then the Holy

---

Hard Questions About Faith

Number Four: Why has no one ever been able to move a mountain? If you cannot take that promise at face value, it comes off as a trick, and doesn't speak well for the rest of Jesus' promises.

Spirit pounces on the situation we have spoken into, applying His power to it.

My congregation was on a campout once when it started to rain just at dinnertime. What a nuisance! I asked the Lord what to do about it.

Tell it to stop, came the reply.

What if I tell it and it doesn't stop? was my immediate thought, of course.

But I decided to pluck up my courage and give it a try. So I called the congregation to form a large circle and hold hands. Looking up, I told the clouds loudly to hold their rain and I commanded the rain to stop. And I invited the people to join me in this rebuke.

Within five minutes the rain stopped!

Does speaking out always have such a quick and dramatic result? No. I have uttered many words that did not come true. So what do we do about that?

Part of faith is the realization that we are beginners at this faith stuff, and that if something does not come off the way we said it should, that God has got the mistake covered and will redeem it. So we can afford to be humble and honest, admitting the mistake and therefore canceling its ongoing destructiveness.

If it had continued to rain, a destructive way of responding would have been to say, "Someone here is nullifying the effectiveness of our words by doubt. He or she is hindering the work of God and had better repent!" That takes a mere mistake and catapults it to the level of a catastrophe of misteaching, disunity and pride.

A more mature response would have been to say something like this: "Well, folks, I thought the Lord wanted us to tell the rain to stop, but it's still raining. We tried our best, but I guess I heard wrong. I'm sorry about that. Meanwhile, to your tents! Let's make the best of this."

Now, what about mountains? I have never heard of a mountain obeying some Christian's command that it move. My assumption is that Jesus was speaking figuratively. In this sense I have seen many mountainous things move.

Mountains are the big things that challenge or oppose us. Despair, opposition, debt and difficulty are some of the mountains I have seen respond to the word of faith. Some of them move fast and some slowly. But they *do* move because our faith releases the muscle of God against them.

Tithing

"Tithing? Are you kidding? What does that have to do with faith?"

A great deal. More than half of Jesus' parables involve money. He Himself claimed that where your money goes is where your heart goes. If you are not investing a significant portion of your funds into God's purposes, you are exempting yourself from a major area in which He displays His grace.

Faith, I have been saying, is a "do" kind of thing, and tithing is a very effective way to do faith. You just write a check to your church—a simple act of trust and commitment.

For those of you who already tithe, that statement is true, isn't it? You have proved it is true by your own experience. For those of you who do not yet tithe, "just write a check" is not simple at all, is it? You can think of all the ways it could go wrong.

I can give you a hundred stories of how tithing has benefited believers, but what I said earlier—understanding follows obedience—is what you need to hear. You will never understand how your faithful act of tithing permits God to bless you, especially financially, until you have done it. Let me give you just one story to encourage you to jump into tithing.

I do not like to talk about money because I think that subject has been overdone in the Church. So I did not preach about it for more than a decade. But last year I preached a series of sermons on money, during which I challenged those who were unemployed to tithe—give ten percent to the Lord—on all money that came into their homes. Six of them did it. And all six were employed within six weeks.

I am not promising you that if you start tithing, your fiscal situation will suddenly turn around. What I am promising is that if you start tithing, you will be freeing God to bless you in ways that relate directly to your entire life, including your finances. Tithing is one of the most effective methods of exercising faith.

Visualizing

Remember what I said about the importance of listening to God? If someone has listened to God, the things that he or she imagines can be a wonderful means of releasing God's power into needs and opportunities. Visualizing—the kind of imagination I am talking about here—is when you actively see in your mind that things change.

You could, for example, close your eyes and "see" this page in this book turn green. Right? If you did that, you would see a faint image of green covering the paper. That is what I mean by active seeing. If you believe that God wants to heal someone's arthritic hands, you may "see" their fingers straightening, becoming normal and working properly. Then you can decide that God's power is at work to achieve that result.

What differentiates this practice from New Age? As you know, there are all sorts of non-Christian forms of spirituality, mostly based in Hinduism, that are being practiced in America today. These practices can be foolish at best and dangerous at worst. At their worst they actively participate in the supernatural power of the devil and his demons, who have nothing but ill will for human beings. You can loose demonic power to affect yourself and others by visualizing what you have heard from an astrologer, spirit guide, séance leader, palm reader or your own natural thoughts.

But because an ability can be misused is no reason to throw it out altogether. We must discipline ourselves to discard any idea that comes from a non-Christian source or is contrary to Scripture. If it suddenly seemed a good idea to you to go to a séance, your knowledge of the Bible would immediately correct that idea. If you do not know the Bible that well, get several translations of the Bible and read Deuteronomy 18:9–13 in each one. That will give you a detailed list of practices to stay away from.

If you are dedicated to listening to and obeying God, your ability to visualize or conceptualize something happening is a powerful vehicle for having faith. Jesus Himself said that He did only what He saw His Father doing (John 5:19); that He taught only what the Father told Him to teach (John 7:16); that He only spoke what the Father told Him to say (John 8:28) and even *how* to say it (John 12:49); and that He was not there for His own agenda but for the Father's (John 7:28). When Jesus went to raise

---

Hard Questions About Faith

Number Five: What is the difference between having the faith of Abraham, calling "things that are not as though they were," and pretend or self-deception? Isn't faith really just a game of spiritual make-believe?

Lazarus from the dead, I suspect He was "seeing" Lazarus alive and well long before He got to the outside of the tomb.

If you present your need to God and listen and He seems to give you direction, then you may see your children performing well on an exam; a check coming in the mail as part of a prayer that God will meet your financial needs; the light of God's healing power gobbling up the

germs causing your cold; a friend coming to belief in Jesus.
You may conceptualize a solution to a problem or hear
alienated friends apologizing to each other.

Seeing, hearing, conceptualizing—these are ways in
which your creative imagination can work. Do not be
afraid to experiment with these abilities. Just determine
that you will refuse to engage in any practice prohibited
by God's Word.

Psalm 143

David the psalmist gave us a wonderful method of having faith in response to troubles. In Psalm 143 he offered
this sequence:

1. *Admit your need:* "The enemy pursues me. . . . My
   spirit grows faint . . . my heart within me is dis-
   mayed" (verses 3–4).
2. *Remember what God has done in the past:* "I remember . . . I meditate on all your works and consider
   what your hands have done" (verse 5).
3. *Ask for God's help:* "I spread out my hands to you"
   (verse 6).
4. *Ask for answers:* "Answer me quickly. . . . Bring me
   word. . . . Show me the way. . . . Rescue me. . . . Teach
   me to do your will" (verses 7–10).

Step #2 is the key to building faith. Recalling what God
has done in the past rekindles our faith for what He can
do in the present. So it is good to spend time remember-
ing the great record of God's mighty acts in the Bible, in
history and in our own lives.

That is exactly what the prophet Habakkuk was doing
when he said, "LORD, I have heard of your fame; I stand in
awe of your deeds, O LORD. Renew them in our day, in our
time make them known" (3:2). Isaiah did the same:

"Awake, awake! Clothe yourself with strength, O arm of the LORD; awake, as in days gone by, as in generations of old. . . . Was it not you who dried up the sea? . . ." (51:9–10).

When we remind God what He has done in the past, faith begins to rise in us for what He might do now.

Faith for Protection

While I was writing this book, the San Fernando Valley, where I live, experienced the great earthquake of January 17, 1994. Even though I was sure the roof was coming down, I had solid peace while the earth heaved. My heart rate did not go up at all. And I knew that everything would turn out O.K. Why?

In chapter 6 I will talk at length about spiritual warfare. For the moment, let it suffice for me to mention one aspect of spiritual warfare: protection. One can easily succumb, in an increasingly dangerous world, to paranoia for oneself or one's family. Here is how my wife, Sue, and I have learned to cope with danger, including the danger of paranoia.

When our children were young, a number of events happened to them that caused Sue and me considerable anxiety. Kevin was robbed twice at knifepoint; David was bitten in the back by a large dog so that when I looked into the wound I could see his lung expanding and contracting; David had his finger cut off; Jason had an accident that cost us two thousand dollars' worth of hand surgery; Joel had a life-threatening bike accident. That list is not complete, but you get the idea.

When I cried out to God in concern for my sons, He led me to Ephesians 6, where Paul states clearly that our enemy is vastly beyond our natural ability to defeat him. (I already knew that.) Paul states just as clearly that we had better avail ourselves, therefore, of the protection of

God. In other words, without God we are sitting ducks, and with God we are an overwhelming majority.

So, using my imagination, I began to "see" Jesus protecting each of my boys every morning. I used several biblical images. I saw a shield around them; I saw them covered with the blood of Jesus and surrounded by the light of His resurrection from the dead; I saw a wide hedge around them keeping evil away. After using my imagination in this way, I would say, "Lord, I now decide that Your protection is on my children. Thank You for looking after them."

I soon found that this is an effective way to have faith. In response to these prayers, serious accidents and other types of harm diminished radically. What's more, events that *should* have turned out badly ended with only minor results. Not only did God's protection keep much evil from occurring, but the enemy's attacks that did occur were turned aside in their severity.

A truly great blessing for Sue and me has been the disappearance of paranoia. As we learned to pray on a regular, daily basis for protection, we have seen God's protective power at work again and again. A consequence of this has been our ability to refuse to allow fear of mishap to impact us. We simply tell anxiety to go away, for God's care and protection are on us and our children.

Having Intimacy with God

Sue had been suffering from a physical condition for several weeks that had not responded to prayer or medical care. My relationship with Jesus, meanwhile, had been developing into one of close and loving intimacy. I spent much time looking at Him in my mind's eye, admiring Him, telling him how much I loved and enjoyed Him.

One night after Sue went to sleep, I was enjoying this closeness just before nodding off myself. As I talked with

Him, He motioned toward Sue, and I knew that power was suddenly available to meet her need. Almost incidentally, I laid my hand on her shoulder and prayed an extremely brief prayer for her healing.

When she awoke in the morning, she was well. She had been healed out of the largess of an intimate relationship with Jesus.

I would promote this method vigorously. As Norman Grubb noted, "He that is joined to the Lord is one spirit." If all power is in Him, therefore, all power is in us. And, wrote Grubb, "We begin to live secretly with God in an invisible world, whose resources become more real to us than the visible."

His Presence Instead of Answers

Up until he died a few months ago, I had been praying vigorously for one of my dearest friends, Chuck. We had known each other for 33 years. He had cancer of the pancreas and liver. When I heard about Chuck's illness, I went to the Lord several times, asking what His will might be. On one occasion I felt the Lord direct me to Psalm 68:20: "Our God is a God who saves; from the Sovereign LORD comes escape from death."

The words *escape from death* burrowed into my soul. A general word had become a particular word—a rhema (as I mentioned in the last chapter), and I was encouraged to pray for Chuck's healing.

A few weeks later, after it was evident that he was not improving, I asked the Lord again, "Do You mean to heal him?"

The reference Ezekiel 33:16 came to mind. I looked up that verse to find these words: "He will surely live."

I decided that the Lord was speaking to me in these two passages and that He wanted me to keep on praying for healing.

In the weeks before Chuck died, there were many signs of God's intervention in the illness: an almost total absence of pain, financial concerns miraculously resolved, answers to Chuck's questions about faith. But he declined steadily toward death.

One day a few months ago, I felt an urging to drive the hundred miles to his city and see him, though Sue and I were scheduled to go the next day. Fifteen minutes after we walked into his hospital room, he died.

I have agonized in the months since then about his death. I have asked a million questions, to which I have received few answers. Why did I think God intended to heal him? Why did those exact passages come to my attention? Why didn't the Lord help me get him and his family more ready for his dying than his healing? Was it that I did not have enough faith? Why didn't it work? Why did he die?

Why, why, why. You know, I have decided something: We do not need the answer to the *why* questions. I suspect the answers would not comfort us anyway, even if we could hear them. What we need is the presence of the Lord. His presence is the answer. He is the comforter.

So I have told Him, "It is You I need. Please come to me." He has. And I am comforted, even though I am not yet answered.

Prayers to Sovereignty

During my devotions one day, I was reading in Psalm 119. When I came to verse 18, I saw these words: "Open my eyes that I may see wonderful things in your law."

Why ask God to open your eyes? I thought. *Why not just open them yourself?*

I dropped the idea and read on. Then in verses 33–37 I met this concept again:

> Teach me, O LORD, to follow your decrees. . . . Give me
> understanding. . . . Direct me in the path of your com-
> mands. . . . Turn my heart toward your statutes. . . . Turn
> my eyes away from worthless things.

I began realizing that the psalmist was asking God to
do things for him that we normally think are our own
responsibility. I began thinking of my failures to reform
myself. I recalled my friend Lloyd saying that "no one can
change his heart; he can only ask God to change it." Then
it dawned on me that there are times we need to pay particular regard to the sovereignty of God and His authoritative ability to do great things—things that are impossible for us.

I am greatly encouraged by the psalmist's example. Following his lead, I have prayed to the sovereign Lord to do
things I am unable to do myself—things I had not dared
to think could be done by anyone, even Him. The result
is that He has accomplished things I would not have even
asked for hitherto. God is sovereign.

I encourage you to pray to His sovereignty: "Change my
heart. Cause me to desire Your will. Direct my feet away
from evil. Turn me toward righteousness."

Thinking on Jesus

This leads me to the next method. What our faith is all
about is Jesus, not answers. Our trust is in Him more than
in anything we expect or need Him to do. He, and nothing or no one else, is our salvation.

This is difficult for us Westerners to grasp because we
are so performance-oriented. "You are what you do" is
almost our summary of personhood. And surely our God
is the God who acts! But it is He Himself more than His
action that we must focus on. Jesus, Hebrews tells us, is
the "author and perfecter of our faith" (Hebrews 12:2). He

is faith's beginning and end, its source and destination, its root and perfecter. We are to "fix our eyes on Jesus," therefore, more than on the thing we need Him to do.

If I get too focused on what I need Him to do, I can become easily misled. I do not have all knowledge and all wisdom. I can easily misdiagnose my need and its solution. So I can put myself in line for a real letdown if I over-focus on the thing I think He needs to do. But if I keep my focus on Him—reminding myself of His power, His kindness, His mercy, His holiness, His knowledge and wisdom and resourcefulness—then I have put my attention where it belongs. David did this again and again. "He alone is my rock and my salvation," he declared. "He is my fortress, I will never be shaken" (Psalm 62:2).

Seventy-five percent of David's psalms reminded the Lord of his enemies. He wanted the Lord to do something about those enemies, of course (and even offered bold suggestions!), but it is clear that David's hope was in the Lord Himself. Over and over he told God "You are my strength."

You will never be misled if you focus on the Lord Himself. Do not put your faith in your faith or in the things you need Him to do, but in *Him*. That kind of faith not only frees Him to act, but it frees Him to sustain you in the absence of His acting, if that is what is needed at the time.

The Lord Himself is more than all answers. It is He as relater rather than actor who must take priority in our hearts. How you relate to Him is vastly more important than what He is doing for you.

And this takes us to our final way to grow faith.

The No-Method Method

Job gives us the example of the no-method method—sheer, grit-your-teeth determination not to give up hope.

He memorialized this attitude when he said, "Though he slay me, yet will I hope in him" (13:15).

George MacDonald wrote:

> The true child, the righteous man, will trust absolutely, against all appearances, the God who has created in him the love of righteousness. God does not, I say, tell Job why he had afflicted him: he rouses his child-heart to trust.

There are times when our agonized questions find no satisfactory answers, when nothing we do makes any difference in our situation, when the situation is past managing, past our ability to endure. Yet somehow we are enabled to take the next step, impossible though it is and hopeless though it is to resolve the dilemma.

> When nothing works,
> when God is silent,
> when others do not help,
> when hope seems foolish,
> when giving up seems the only recourse,
> when you are fatigued and have no prospect of rest,
> when confusion reigns,
> stand.
> That's all.
> Just stand.

"And after you have done everything . . . stand," Paul said to the Ephesians (6:13). Just standing is success. Refusing to be pushed over. Not going ahead, but not being pushed back either. That's the no-method method. It works, because God backs it up.

Summary

I have shared with you in this chapter more than a dozen methods by which we can grow faith. Be patient with me when I remind you again that it is not the methods that work, but God who works. We do not put faith in our faith; we put faith in God who makes our faith effective.

These methods are taught by God in Scripture, however, and I have found them invaluable in nurturing faith in our great God.

The next page begins the third major section of this book, in which we will look at present-day obstacles to the business of having faith.

Part **3**

Current Enemies of Faith

Now we begin a very different approach to the business of having faith. This is the time to think about putting up your guard, for factors are at work in the world that see your faith as a dangerous enemy. Some of these factors are cultural, some are merely personal, some come from the enemy of our souls, some even originate in the misteachings of the Christian Church. All these factors can undermine, even sabotage the successful operation of your faith, so we must gird ourselves by examining them.

You may find some of the following material a bit heady, a skosh too intellectual. Never mind. Just chew your way through it, eating what is meat for you and spitting out the bones.

5
Cultural Conditionings

Truth requires a context. It is always true to say, "Jesus is Lord," but in order for it to make sense we must apply that statement to a context. What good is it to say, "Jesus is Lord" without aiming that truth at a personal, economic, political, social, psychological or some other context?

Contexts are always changing. It is in the nature of reality to change because reality is dynamic; it affects things. The application of truth, therefore, is also constantly changing. That is why we have to keep reading and writing new books.

Culture is one of the contexts to which reality must be addressed. It is not enough for a parent to tell his child, "When I was your age . . ." because there have been such monumental cultural changes that the child could rightly respond, "You were never my age!"

In every culture, at all times, there is a battle for the mind—for what people think and do not think, believe and do not believe. In this chapter we will look at several cultural factors that are especially important today (more than yesterday) in the business of having faith. As I said, this may be stiffer stuff intellectually than one normally encounters in a popular work. But it is crucial that we get a grasp on these concepts and understand what has been going on.

Worldview

Here are some statements about a very important cultural consideration. James Sire gives us the simplest definition of worldview:

> A worldview is a set of presuppositions (or assumptions) which we hold (consciously or unconsciously) about the basic make-up of our world.

Paul Hiebert states it this way:

> At the center of a culture is its "worldview"—the fundamental way it organizes and perceives the world. . . . This "core" is made up of:
> 1) existential assumptions about what exists and how it is organized
> 2) affective assumptions about the nature of feelings
> 3) normative assumptions about the nature of values, priorities, and allegiances.

Charles Kraft wraps up the idea in this fashion:

> Cultures pattern perceptions of reality into conceptualizations of what reality can or should be, what is to be regarded as actual, probable, possible, and impossible. These conceptualizations form what is termed the "worldview" of the culture. The worldview is the central sys-

tematization of conceptions of reality to which the members of the culture assent (largely unconsciously) and from which stems their value system. The worldview lies at the very heart of the culture, touching, interfacing with, and strongly influencing every aspect of culture.

What these scholars are describing—a filtering system by which people both see and interpret their world—is a cultural dynamic of immense importance. I believe it is *the* major factor in international diplomacy (politics, business, religion, military involvement and educational exchange), in racism, even in male-female miscommunication.

Notice that Sire and Kraft use the word *unconscious.* One's worldview prompts one to make unconscious assumptions about oneself and others. This means that we debate our opinions not straightforwardly but obliquely because they are not sitting on the surface where we can see them.

Many indicators suggest that the worldview of the United States is going to change. Thank God! The considerable influx of non-Europeans into our society, the shrinking of worldwide communications, our expanding contact with other cultures through travel and various modes of exchange, and the unraveling of our current societal values are all contributors to the changing of our worldview. And not a moment too soon.

Where Did Our Worldview Come From?

Our worldview came to us through a European process in which assumptions became rationalized. Descartes got this process well underway with his statement "I think, therefore I am." The acceptance of that deduction placed the intellect in an unbalanced ascendancy in Western civilization that has yet to be corrected. It also began a devaluing of the human spirit and its apparently less rational functions of intuition, imagination and conscience. A century later this process culminated in what we call the Enlightenment.

The values of the Enlightenment were *rationalism, learning, skepticism* and *empiricism.* Let's look briefly at these four values:

1. *Rationalism* is the principle and practice of accepting reason as the sole authority in determining one's opinions or course of action.
2. *Learning* is the acquisition of knowledge and skill.
3. *Skepticism* is the assumption that the truth of all knowledge must always be in question and that inquiry is tantamount to a process of doubting.
4. *Empiricism* is the search for knowledge by observation and experimentation with the assumption that sensory experience is the only true source of knowledge.

The plus side of Enlightenment thinking is the benefits that have come to the world through the scientific method. Modern medicine, telecommunications, mechanical inventions and products, increased productivity, even managerial expertise are a short list of blessings that come from the use of the scientific method. The world would be a vastly poorer place without the blessings of the Enlightenment.

But let's look at the negative side. Picture a line between God and humankind:

God

Humankind

The Enlightenment assumes that if God exists, man can deduce, observe, prove and verify His existence by rational and empirical means that should be able to stand the test of skepticism. "Can't poor old God take a little scrutiny?" as someone once asked mockingly. In any case, it is up to human beings to pierce the line between God and man by themselves, from beneath.

But since human beings can *not* pierce that line, guess what? The line does not exist and neither does God, who apparently does not sit on the other side of it after all.

That is the best that enlightened thinking can do, for when reason is one's god, a rationally unverifiable god is no god at all.

A scriptural worldview, by contrast, holds that God is the only one who can pierce the line, and that His piercing of it is called revelation. *Everything* we know about God comes from His revelation of Himself to us. All information about Him—in nature, in Scripture, in church life, in our devotional relationship with Him, in anything at all—comes through revelation. This is true of information that comes to the human race in general and to us as individuals. What was revealed to Isaiah must also be revealed to *me* in order for me to profit from it. What's more (reflecting what we discussed in chapter 2), it is not primarily the intellect to which God reveals Himself, but the spirit. (The spirit in human beings, remember, is the site of input from God, like the receiver in a TV set.)

To the rationalist, neither the Holy Spirit nor the human spirit exists, since neither is rationally verifiable. But this says more about the rationalist's worldview than about reality. Because his worldview operates largely unconsciously, the rationalist is unaware of its force in his life. The factor that exercises the most influence is the least examined (which itself is hardly a rational position!). When the rationalist runs into a different worldview, he dismisses it as superstition or myth instead of giving it the possibility of credibility. Thus, the spiritual arena remains unexplored.

The matter of worldview is what makes the Westerner's thinking so unintelligible to the Buddhist or Hindu or animist or Muslim or third-world Christian, for their worldviews include the existence of spirits, curses, mediums, angels, heaven and hell, God and devils, healings and foreknowledge. They do not question the existence of these spiritual entities. They question, rather, how to use them for their benefit and protect themselves from their threats. They think of the Westerner as naïve, while the Westerner thinks of them as superstitious. And the Westerner's question "Who is right?" reflects more a worldview assumption than a true resolution of the disparity.

Is Your Worldview an Enemy of Your Faith?

Let me ask you a question: Are there occurrences in the Bible that you doubt really took place? If so, you may be influenced more than you realize by an Enlightenment worldview. Most of the occurrences we have trouble with are those related to natural phenomena—the very things that Enlightenment thinking is most emphatic about.

Great numbers of Christians in the West, for example, do not consider prayer as a serious response to illness until it becomes obvious that medical science cannot fix it. Then faith in the—what do we call it? *super*natural— begins to exhibit itself, but often as a last-ditch resort, which is hardly the best starting point for growth in faith in the God of miracles.

Remember, obedience precedes understanding. Let me expand that statement. Willful obedience precedes intellectual understanding. God is not opposed to intellectual understanding, but understanding is the result of faith rather than the reason for it.

O.K., here's the point. If your worldview dismisses godly possibilities, it is an enemy of your faith. That sounds all right, doesn't it? Let me state it in a tougher way: If your insistence on being sure, on validating research and on taking responsible action prevents you from obeying God, then your worldview is an enemy of your faith.

What? Being sure is being responsible, isn't it? What if everybody went popping off doing whatever they felt like? No, that is not faith either. But the insistence on being sure makes an end-run around the requirement for faith. Again: "Without faith it is impossible to please God, because anyone who comes to him must believe that he exists and that he rewards those who earnestly seek him" (Hebrews 11:6). The verse does not say, "Anyone who comes to Him must have verified His existence" or, "Must have researched His existence adequately" or, "Must be sure that He exists." In fact, to insist on being sure is to *not* please Him. It is faith, not certainty, that pleases God. Do you see? Our Western worldview—which looks so responsible and adult and mature—is one of the primary foes of effective faith!

This may be upsetting. Some readers may be beginning to question this now: "He sounded O.K. a while back but this is a bit much." I know I'm not Jesus, but they said the same thing about Him when He was rattling their world-view big-time in John 6. They thought He was command-ing them to engage in cannibalism, and He let them think it, telling them (rather slyly) to believe instead of being sure. "Does this offend you?" He asked. "... The Spirit gives life; the flesh counts for nothing" (John 6:61, 63).

Jesus knew good and well He was offending them. He also knew that faith, not clarification, was what had to resolve the matter for them. Verse 66 says that many of them left. We must surmise that He let them go, since He could easily have resolved their worldview objections in order to retain their following. To Him, then, that they trusted Him was apparently more important than that they continued to follow Him. In Jesus' worldview, you see, obedience precedes understanding.

One might ask, Do I make Jesus explain before I believe? Well, recall what He said to the Twelve after the troubled people took off: "Do you also wish to go away?" (John 6:67, NRSV). If He was willing to let *them* go away, do you think He would do any differently with us?

I think the first sentence of Peter's reply indicates that they wanted to leave but realized their other options were worse: "Lord, to whom shall we go? You have the words of eternal life. We believe and know that you are the Holy One of God" (verses 68–69). Then Jesus gave them no help at all: "Have I not chosen you, the Twelve? Yet one of you is a devil!" (verse 70). That sounds for all the world like a lack of confidence to me!

And note that Jesus still did not resolve the cannibalism revulsion of their worldview. He had said they had to eat His flesh, and did not clarify it (that we know of) until the Last Supper when He finally identified His body with thankfully consumable bread. They must have heaved a huge sigh of relief! Meanwhile, they had passed a test of faith, for they had stayed with Him even though they were repulsed by His teaching and had not yet been given a satisfactory resolution to it. They had taken the clue "the Spirit gives life" and allowed the Spirit to give them peace even though they had not yet received intellectual resolution.

Our worldview may keep us from God. Our faith can allow us to follow Him. When there is a crunch, go with your faith.

Philosophical Underpinnings

The next cultural factor I want to address is an especially tragic result of the worldview of the Enlightenment—its impact on the philosophical base of our society.

A worldview that values rationalism, learning, skepticism and empiricism could coexist only so long with a Judeo-Christian worldview before a major conflict occurred. The reason: Worldviews spawn philosophies. A philosophy is a worldview writ large. It is the spelling out of the values of the worldview in terms of aesthetics, ethics, logic or metaphysics. In the West in the eighteenth century, Judeo-Christian theologies (the philosophies of a biblical worldview) began to be contested by rationalism. At some point these two philosophies parted company on the most basic of premises: Reality is either God-centered or man-centered; it cannot be both. God-centered philosophies are Judeo-Christian, man-centered philosophies humanistic.

Ownership of the body and its functions is one major philosophical conflict that produces all kinds of personal and societal behaviors. Let's look, for purposes of illustration, at suicide. As I write these words, the name Jack Kevorkian makes the newspapers regularly because he keeps helping people to commit suicide and defending the right to do it. "Human beings," says a humanist like Kevorkian, "have a right *not* to suffer. It's no one's business but mine what I do or don't do with my own body. If I want to end my life, it's my concern, whether or not it's a good decision by anyone else's criteria." Indeed, if human beings are at the center of life, this proposition makes sense.

In a God-centered philosophy, God is the determiner of life. "The earth is the LORD's, and everything in it" (Psalm 24:1). "You are not your own; you were bought at a price" (1 Corinthians 6:19–20). It is the Lord's decision when we die. We do not have the right to usurp His timing and kill ourselves, even when suffering is involved. What's more, Christianity claims that it is for our benefit, whether that benefit is noticeable at the moment or not, that we leave the time and manner of our death to God. Even more, it is for the benefit of society—which Scripture holds more important than the welfare of the individual—that God determine the details of our death.

Humanism is not only man-centered but *individualistically* man-centered; that is, the rights of the individual take precedence over the rights of the community. To the observations of common sense, this is counterproductive to society. Nonetheless the courts of our land—the citadel for humanism—hand down decisions regularly that are socially abortive. Legal decisions concerning criminals, pregnancy and sexuality have tipped the boat of our society to the brink of capsizing.

What does this have to do with faith? Four things, at least.

First, God will not bless a decision that runs counter to His will—even a decision made with care, integrity and compassion. Care, integrity and compassion have been prominent in some of the most ludicrous court decisions (the fellow who was awarded $200,000 from his parents, for example, because they did not abort him when they learned of his pre-birth congenital deformity).

Second, humanism appears to take the high moral ground. Bright, articulate spokespersons have made important Judeo-Christian positions look biased, uninformed, cold, outdated and unmanageable. But it has always been so. Christians appeal to a different understanding of reality, with different faculties. It is understandable that we want to be understood, but it is a futile hope because only faith will enable those who oppose us to comprehend us. So we must resist the impact of the influence of humanism while maintaining a proactive faith and behavior that promote the causes of God.

This does not mean there is no room for dialogue between Christians and non-Christians about societal issues. While the faith is transrational, it is rational to many who are able to respond to clear thinking. But the Christian must remember that faith is a dynamic that, at heart, transcends the ability of the merely rational to comprehend.

Third, believers must keep going to the Bible and to the Holy Spirit for the truth and for the application of truth to complex contemporary situations. It takes the Bible *and* the Spirit, for the Spirit is both the author and the interpreter of Scripture.

Without the Spirit, one can read the Word in a legalistic, death-dealing manner in which even the letter of the New Testament kills. "He has made us competent as ministers of a new covenant—not of the letter but of the Spirit; for the letter kills, but the Spirit gives life" (2 Corinthians 3:6). Have you ever seen someone use the Bible in a way that produced not life but death? That comes from reading the Word without welcoming the Spirit's influence.

Without the agreement of God's Word, on the other hand, one can assume that a message from the Holy Spirit is genuine when it is not and end up seriously misled. "Test the spirits," John exhorts us (1 John 4:1). Charismatics can be prone to such confidence in the Spirit's guidance that they do not use the Bible to check that guidance. Much woe can be eliminated by a humble exposure of one's guidance to the scrutiny of the Word.

Fourth, let's not turn over the whole enterprise of philosophy to the humanists. We need Christian philosophers—people who can articulate the faith in such fashion that debaters are encouraged to believe for themselves. Paul's interaction with the philosophers in Athens is a good model. But remember, they will never come to God on purely intellectual grounds. You must use your mind to address their spirits.

Timing

You might think that timing is relatively insignificant in a discussion of culture and faith. Let me invite you to think again.

We are affected by a changing sense of timing every time we sit down before a TV or venture outside to drive a car or wait for service in a business establishment. Each of us has a vastly different opinion from a decade ago of *how long* something should take. Feelings and thoughts of impatience are quick to appear these days.

Surely God is intensely aware of our sense of timing. But He is not swayed by it. Having attended to such minute details as the number of hairs on our heads since our last shampoo, He is worthy and capable of determining the exact *when* as well as the exact *how* of His responses to our faith. He reserves to Himself—in full knowledge of our circumstances, our history, our temperament, our needs, our everything—the timing of His response to our faith.

"The world too much is with us," Wordsworth observed, but it is not too much with God. That is, He rules it rather than is ruled by it. God's sense of timing is perfect. It may not feel perfect to us, conditioned as we are to instant everything, but it is perfect nonetheless. God may wait until 11:59, as many have lamented, but He is never a minute late. (I must confess to you that I have had to reset my watch several times when I was on a wait for God. I kept thinking that midnight had come and passed, but I was wrong.)

Remember the analogy of the muscle. Waiting is stretching, exercising the muscle of faith. And you know what? *He* decides how long will be most beneficial for you to wait. So part of our faith must be to come to the point where we say to Him: "O.K., Lord, You know how I feel about this waiting, but I willfully trust that You know when to answer my need. You are kind and capable and have my best interests at heart, so I can trust that You are not playing with me in some heartless cat-and-mouse game, but yearning with all Your heart to bless me. I will wait for You to come through."

Easy and Hard

The next cultural factor I want to look at is something so ingrained in our expectations that we may miss its threat to our exercise of faith. I am speaking of our notions of how easy or hard something is.

Our culture has put an ascending value over the past couple of decades on easiness. Small wonder! What we call "labor-saving devices" manage to extract an amazing amount of energy from us in payment for the labor they perform. And often it is at just the wrong moment that they go bust! The demands we are expected to meet are greater than the demands these labor-saving devices replaced. So multiplied have become the demands on us that many of us are ready to shout, "Stop!" Sometimes just one more phone call is enough to send us over the edge of self-control or civility or hope. Someone might fume, "Jesus Christ better come soon because I'm going to wear out if He doesn't. Don't tell me life is easy!"

We might as well confess it: We are just a bit spoiled. If you have ever used a public telephone in a third-world country, you realize how easy we in the U.S. have it. And what do we do in that third-world place? We judge it. Even if we are gentle, we criticize what we consider inferior, assuming that *our* standard is the real standard of what should be. Because it is easy for us at home, it should be easy for us there. When it is not, we chafe, feeling a tiny bit martyrish.

I am being foolish, of course, but tolerate me for a moment by taking seriously this question: What if God were a Nigerian educator? We in the West assume that education should be formal, outside the home and teacher-centered. We promote learning by creating formal schools and hiring specialists to run them. Nigerians, on the other hand, assume that education is primarily informal, inside the home and learner-centered. They promote learning by doing, discipleship and using proverbs and folk tales. It is nutty, no doubt, but what if God liked the Nigerian way of educating in preference to ours? What would that preference do to your concept of easiness and hardness? What if you sensed that God almighty wanted you to educate your children in the Nigerian style? What would that do to your faith?

You would have to make serious adjustments concerning priorities, attitudes about what is really important and your expenditure of time and energy. You would have to deal with your own belief system; with your control over your own time; with changing behaviors with your kids. It would be hard, wouldn't it? In fact, it would be so hard that you might be tempted to refuse to comply with God's wishes.

What is my point? That we need to submit our concepts of easiness and hardness, like our concepts of timing, to the Lordship of the Lord. He knows what He wants. He knows that what He wants is best for us. He knows the exact details of our responses to His will. He knows precisely how to get us from point A to point B and on what schedule.

Are these things not so? You see, God *is* a Nigerian educator, whether He does or does not want you to be one. He is learner-centered. That is, He is *you*-centered. He has arranged the details of your personal life (not just your professional life). He wants to teach you in your own home. He chooses to be informal, friendly, casual with you (rather than formal, distant and impersonal). He wants to come alongside you (rather than lecture you), working with and through you as you learn the skills of life and relationships. He wants to tell you stories more than facts, and cultivate character more than knowledge.

He wants you to be able to say to the Father, along with Jesus, "I have brought you glory on earth by completing the work you gave me to do" (John 17:4). There was still a lot of work to be done, of course, but not by Jesus. He did all and only what the Father told him to do; the rest was for others to accomplish.

What does He want you to do? This question includes, of course, what does He *not* want you to do. Can you trust Him to cover all the bases that need covering? He will cover some of them through you, but some of them through others. Can you trust Him not to fatigue you? Not to abuse you? Not to manipulate you? Can you accept that He knows everything He has appointed you to do, and refuse, therefore, to add your own stuff to His "to do" list?

Have you ever been stretched by being given something too easy to do? That is just how our God works. I suspect that most of us are stretched more by what is easy than by what is hard. Do not let your culture establish your job description. God knows you and your culture better than you, and can be trusted to thread your way through it.

Success and Failure

From the foregoing, you can assume that I am going to say something similar about success and failure. You're right. Only God can truly define what constitutes success and failure. We are study-ridden and study-idolatrous, and the Enlightenment values of research and verification make fools of us.

I read in the newspaper just today that the latest study says sugar does *not* make children hyperactive. If that is true, I need to apologize to two of my sons for depriving them unnecessarily. But if it is not true, I do not have to worry. Rather than wait until all the studies come to agreement, I can decide to trust God to know the truth and lead me accordingly. I can change the basis of my decision-making from studies to God.

You know by now that I am not saying God is opposed to studies. He just does not like them taking His place.

After first reading about cholesterol, I asked God if I should change my eating habits. His reply was *Sort of.* "In a general way," He was saying, "you could profit from eating less fat. But don't let fatless food become an idol. *I* have appointed the number of your days. Trust Me more than the studies to ensure that you live out all of them."

In heaven the heroes will likely be people whose names never made the headlines on earth. They will be people who listened to and obeyed God, trusting in His direction for their lives and ignoring the influence of their culture.

The Big Lie

The big lie used to have a single expression: "If it is not logical, it is not so." But the human potential movements of the last third-of-a-century have added another version: "If you don't feel it, it is not so." It makes sense in a man-centered philosophy to postulate that our minds or our emotions are the verifiers of truth. This is ratio-empiricism gone tilt. Since your conclusions and feelings may differ from mine, we are forced to concede that truth is relative instead of absolute.

In a God-centered world, truth is determined by what God says. I do not have to sacrifice intellectual or emotional integrity to acknowledge that a truth may be beyond my comprehension or in conflict with my feelings.

I advised a woman once to forgive her ex-husband.

"I'd be lying if I said I forgave him," she replied.

"Why do you say that?"

"Because I don't feel forgiving toward him."

"You don't have to feel it. Just decide to forgive him and let your feelings come along when they do."

She decided to try it. A couple of weeks later she told me she was now beginning to feel forgiveness toward him.

"If you faith it," I proverbalized, "you will feel it. But if you wait to feel it, you may never faith it."

The big lie immobilizes people in their own integrity.

Summary

As you read the newspaper for the next few weeks, ask yourself if you can detect any worldview assumptions, any God-centered or human-centered attitudes, even any subtle ideas about timing and difficulty. Look for any cultural factors lying in the background of your life that may be exerting a powerful influence against your faith.

In the next chapter we will look at spiritually based opposition to our having faith.

6
Spiritual Attacks

I have concluded over the past twenty years that spiritual warfare is the primary dynamic going on in the world. This fits with a profound observation C. S. Lewis made in *Christian Reflections* about the nature of conflict between God and Satan: "There is no neutral ground in the universe: every square inch, every split second, is claimed by God and counterclaimed by Satan." When it comes to the business of having faith, spiritual warfare really heats up.

St. Paul taught that faith is a shield "with which you can extinguish all the flaming arrows of the evil one" (Ephesians 6:16). If this is so, then faith is *the* primary human target for Satan to attack. He will do all he can to deceive us about how to have faith. He will try to scare us or tempt us or discourage us from exercising our faith.

When Paul wrote Ephesians, he was probably chained to a soldier, so the image of warfare was right at hand.

A Roman soldier used two different shields. The *aspis*, a small, round shield about two feet across, was used in hand-to-hand combat to ward off the opponent's blow while the soldier got ready to swing his own weapon. But the shield Paul mentions here is the *thureon,* a heavy, iron "T" suspending two thick planks, four by two and a half feet overall, behind which the soldier crouched during an artillery barrage.

The shield protected him from arrows about twenty inches long, the tips of which had been laced with hemp, dipped in burning tar and then launched. These arrows, if not stopped, would slam into the soldier's flesh. When the arrow was extracted, the molten tar would remain in the wound, burning a widening hole and further debilitating the soldier. Tacitus counted over three hundred of them in one soldier's shield after a battle. It was vicious, effective warfare. But the shield, sometimes covered with water-soaked leather, would stop the arrow and quench the fire, preventing both the steel and the tar from hurting the soldier.

We have felt those arrows, haven't we? When the steel of sin has been extracted, many of us still have to deal with the tar of continuing shame. On other occasions, the steel of sin does not penetrate our flesh, but we are burned by the tar of accusation—feeling guilty, perhaps, just for having been tempted. The enemy has a veritable arsenal of flaming arrows to fire at us: fear, confusion and anger; hurt, shame and lust; depression, illness and accident; mayhem, attack and poverty. But the promise of the Bible is that *all* these arrows can be quenched by faith.

I want to look at five arrows and how we can raise faith against them to quench them.

1. Temptation

Why does temptation threaten faith? Because to sin breaks our fellowship with God, without which we cannot have faith. Successful temptation is a double threat:

1. It tears our fellowship with God.
2. It cuts us off from Him who supplies our faith.

Let's talk about temptation in two phases.

To Keep Temptation from Succeeding

Satan has been at the business of tempting far longer than we have been at the business of resisting it. He is indeed a roaring lion seeking someone to devour. One of his chief stratagems is to induce us to think we must resist temptation on our own.

A Sunday school teacher once asked a class of nine-year-olds, "What would you do if Satan knocked on your front door?" After a pause one girl responded, "I'd send Jesus to answer the door!" That child knew for certain that she was no match for Satan, but that Jesus was more than his match and that she would have to have His help.

Isn't that precisely what St. Paul implies? "God is faithful; he will not let you be tempted beyond what you can bear. But when you are tempted, he will also provide a way out so that you can stand up under it" (1 Corinthians 10:13).

I once experienced a visitation of grace about this very matter. Like most men, I tend to have trouble with my eyes, looking at women for gratification rather than for blessing. One day as I drove to the bank, I noticed that the sidewalks were lined with figures in skirts. The bank was full of them, too. I almost felt like counting the ceiling tiles so as not to be tempted to look at them.

When I got back to the church, I barged into the empty sanctuary asking, "What am I supposed to do out there? Wear blinders?"

In a flash Jesus asked me three questions:

1. *Was I ever successfully tempted?*

"No, Lord," I replied. "The Scriptures are clear that You never sinned."

2. *Am I in you?*

"Yes, Lord, the Scriptures are also clear that if I've asked You in, You're in."

3. *Why don't you put those two together?*

"You mean You're willing to resist temptation for me, on my behalf?"

Yes.

From that moment, whenever I became aware that I was being tempted, I would sort of motion to Jesus, as though He were at my side, point to the temptation and say, "Go sic 'em, Lord." And He would. The temptation would immediately begin to recede and be completely gone within minutes.

I'm telling you, this was victory! For the first time in my life, I began to relax my fears of being tempted, realizing that I did not *have* to sin. Jesus was there every single time waiting for me to put Him to work resisting the temptation. I would go for weeks at a time without committing many kinds of sins.

For about fifteen years I practiced this form of resisting temptation with good success. The only times I got into trouble were when I delayed sending Jesus against the temptation. He would not attack it until I asked Him, and at times I flirted with the temptation too long before deploying Him against it. At times like that I ended up sinning because I had allowed the temptation to hook me.

Finally—finally!—I became aware that I still loved sin. I was resisting temptation pretty steadily but had to admit, if I was honest, that I still loved the sins I was avoiding. I must tell you that it took *years* to come to this point. What's more, in those years I scorned the idea of holiness as an impossibility, and criticized holiness teachings that were not as mature or honest as they might have been.

Finally I began to pray like this: "Lord, I admit that I love sin. Please change my heart. Give me Your hatred of sin and Your love of holiness. Let me see holiness as You see it."

Within days He began to answer that prayer. He is still answering. And I am having less and less trouble with temptation.

When Temptation Has Succeeded

Conscience is a function of our spirit and works in two ways.

Before we sin conscience says, "Don't do it!" We may experience this as a rapidly spreading emptiness or unrest in our chest. It may be accompanied by physical phenomena like accelerated heart rate, adrenaline surges, flush on the face. We experience this as we come to a point of decision—to do the sin or not.

When temptation has succeeded and we sin, conscience says, "You shouldn't have done it!" We feel remorse, heaviness, mental dullness and a kind of ache over disappointing God and ourselves.

This is *not* punishment! Hear this: It is not punishment. God punished One on a cross in Jerusalem for the sins of all mankind. He is not interested in punishing you. You do not qualify for divine punishment anyhow. For that you have to be the Spirit-sired, sinless Son of God. Only He qualified to be a sacrifice for sin. Only in Him was sin effectively punished. A guilty conscience is not punitive; it is to motivate you to seek forgiveness, to begin the process of restoring the relationship with God that your sin broke.

But the devil is not through with you when you have yielded to temptation. Now he switches tactics and unloads condemnation on you. Condemnation casts you down whereas conviction lifts you up. That is the difference between the post-sin roles of Satan and God. What

Satan wants you to do is bury yourself in self-condemnation. Instead of running to your Forgiver, he wants you to take your medicine and manfully or womanfully bite the bullet and decide you are going to suffer the consequences of your sin. Sounds responsible, doesn't it? It is not. To try to make it right yourself is to perpetuate the consequences of your sin: separation from God.

You cannot make it right. Only the blood of Jesus can do that, and it already did it. All you can do is confess, receive forgiveness and forgive yourself. This is humbling. No amount of breast-beating, self-scourging or self-condemnation will make the least bit of difference to your guilt. Grace alone will remove it. When you have sinned, the only thing is to admit it, the quicker the better, willfully claim that He has forgiven you and willfully tell yourself that you have forgiven you, too.

Will you then *feel* forgiven? Eventually. God knows when. But don't wait to feel it in order to faith it.

You know, some of the best, most anointed, most powerful sermons I have preached have come within twenty-four hours of my worst sins. God is so eager to forgive, so eager to restore, so blessed to pour forth mercy, that He pulls out all the stops to affirm His love for us.

After one Sunday like that, I said to Him, "You're shameless! How dare You use someone like me! No wonder people said to St. Paul that since Your grace abounds in response to sin, maybe we ought to sin more flagrantly."

I say this, of course, not to promote sin but to celebrate forgiveness. The first title for the Church ought to be the Community of the Forgiven, and Sundays ought to be Parties Celebrating Forgiveness.

2. Accusation

The very name *Satan* means "adversary." One of the chief functions of an adversary is to accuse. Scripture specifically labels Satan as "the accuser of our brothers" (Revelation 12:10). In the Scriptures he seems to take particular delight in accusing the righteous and committed rather than the sinful. He does accuse sinners, of course, as I noted in the last section, unloading condemnation on them. But he reserves his sharpest accusations for those who are resisting him successfully.

I have observed that Satan launches the burning arrow of accusation against us on three different occasions.

When We Are Resisting Temptation Successfully

If Satan cannot get us to sin by tempting us, he switches tactics and accuses us. What does he accuse us of? Of having the temptation! *He* puts a thought in our minds—the temptation—and if we resist it, he follows it up with an accusation: *Nasty you! Don't you feel guilty for having had that thought?*

He uses our own thinking processes and vocabularies and feelings to do this, so that often we are unaware that he is at work at all. We think it is simply our own conscience accusing us.

Satan even quotes Scripture at us if he thinks he can get away with it. After all, that's what he tried on Jesus. It works something like this:

1. Satan: *Look at that girl. Don't you wonder what she would be like in bed?*
2. Me: "Lord, I resist the temptation to look wrongly at that girl. Make the enemy leave."
3. Satan: *Don't you feel guilty for having had that thought?*
4. Me: "I resist that accusation."
5. Satan: *Too late! Jesus Himself said that you're just as guilty if you sin in your heart as if you actually do it.*

6. Me: "I rebuke the accusation that I am guilty just for being tempted."

7. Jesus makes the accuser flee.

It is at point #5 that many of us tumble into the hands of the accuser. Listen, being tempted is no sin. If it were, Jesus would be the worst sinner of all, for as Hebrews tells us, He "has been tempted in every way, just as we are—yet was without sin" (4:15). The accuser, masquerading as a messenger of light, sounds reasonable when he accuses us of being tempted, but it is all a lie. Remember, as Jesus warned, "He is a liar and the father of lies" (John 8:44). If you let him lie to you, if you accept false guilt for sin you have not committed, the result is the same as if you *had* sinned: a sense of separation from God. You are not guilty, but you believe you are, so you experience distance from God.

Rebuke the devil firmly for accusations. The promise of Scripture is that if you resist him, he must flee from you.

When Significant Ministry Draws Near

Teams from my church have led more than 130 conferences in various parts of the world (as I mentioned in chapter 1). Anytime from six to two weeks before a conference, we come under attack from the devil. One of his attacks is accusation. What he is trying to do is get us to believe that we are not qualified to do this ministry. He knows us pretty well, so he will take something that contains a measure of truth to get us to doubt our ability to be used in ministry.

- If we are inexperienced, he will say, *Who do you think you are, you big phony! You don't even know what you're doing. You're trying to deceive those people into believing you're an expert.*

- He will say, *It hasn't been long enough since your last big sin for you to do this ministry.* There he is trying to play on our past guilt.
- He will accuse us of not having prepared adequately.
- He will claim that we are not prayed up enough to do this.
- He will even accuse us of details over which we have absolutely no control, except to bow out of the ministry—details such as: *You're too young. It's not your fault, but you have to be at least ten years older before you're equipped to do this.*
- *You haven't got your own flesh under control.*
- *God will expose your feet of clay, just as you've always feared He would, and you'll deserve it.*
- *You're not pure enough, good enough, trained enough, mature enough,* [you-fill-in-the-blank] *enough.*

Whatever Satan can say to cast doubt on you and in you is what he will use. *He uses a half-truth to make a full lie.* The lie is this: *You cannot perform this ministry.*

Now, how should we respond to these accusations? Well, what did Jesus advise? "Agree with your adversary quickly" (Matthew 5:25, NKJV).

"What? Am I supposed to agree with what you just called lies?" Well, not exactly. But we can let accusations drive us to the Lord, for the Lord has the right answer for every accusation. Let's look at the accusations I noted above and possible responses to them.

- *Who do you think you are, you big phony! You don't even know what you're doing. You're trying to deceive those people into believing you're an expert.*
  "He's right, Lord. I'm not nearly experienced enough, but You are, and this reminds me to depend absolutely on You."

- *It hasn't been long enough since your last big sin for you to do this ministry.*

  "How foolish of the devil to remind me of sin, Lord, for this drives me to confess any outstanding sin and bring it under Your grace; or to remind myself that I have already confessed past sins, so they are, according to Hebrews 8:12, dismissed from Your memory."

- *You haven't prepared adequately.*

  "Lord, I've prepared as well as time and circumstances have permitted, and I'm now asking You to bless those preparations and extend their effect far beyond what I've put into them."

- *You're not prayed up enough to do this.*

  "How true, Lord! But Your graciousness is to answer prayers far out of proportion to the effort put into them. This isn't about our efforts, Lord, but Yours. Thank You that You will come through."

- *You're too young. It's not your fault, but you have to be at least ten years older before you're equipped to do this.*

  "Lord, You know my coming in and my going out. You have been at work in my life since my conception. I am weak but You are strong. Show Yourself strong through my weakness, Lord."

- *You haven't got your own flesh under control.*

  "Ah, gracious Lord Jesus, it is Your righteousness that I lay claim to, not my own. It is Christ in us who is the hope of glory, not us. So I'm going on into this, Lord, trusting You to manifest Your character through me."

- *God will expose your feet of clay, just as you've always feared He would, and you'll deserve it.*

  "My Lord, You can deal with me any way You please, for I know that You are kind and loving and merciful and full of compassion toward me. I will trust in Your dealings with me rather than allow the enemy to push me into fearing and running from You."

- *You're not pure enough, good enough, trained enough, mature enough,* [you-fill-in-the-blank] *enough.*

"Oh, buzz off, Satan! I trust God, not you. O Lord, You've gotten me into this and You'll get me through it. Thanks be to God!"

What I have learned over years of dealing with this kind of stuff is that the devil gets increasingly subtle and clever in his accusations. He can always find a new door through which to approach us. We find success not in relying on past success in resisting him but in relying on Jesus, who is the Source of our past success. Let the accuser propel you into the arms of Jesus. Jesus is our defense, our protector, our advocate, our lawyer pleading our cause with the Father and against the adversary. Let Him do His work for you.

When God Is Silent

Mature Christians down through the ages testify to the periodic silence of God. At exceedingly mature levels this has been referred to as "the dark night of the soul." We need not imagine that we are great saints just because we experience a bit of silence from God, but His silences toward us are of the same order as those toward them. The goal of His silence is growth and glory for us; the methodology is that of a test. For some it is the worst test of all, for the enemy is allowed to rant at us continually while God declines to speak.

Satan batters us, of course, with plausible-sounding reasons for the silence of God: We have terminally offended Him; we have finally crossed the line; we are being rebuked for our sins; He does not really care for us because He does not answer our agonized complaints; we do not really matter in the scheme of things; there is no God, we have just been kidding ourselves with child-ish fantasies; if God were truly loving, He would have answered us by now; etc. Doubt is cast alternately at us and at God: We are the problem, God is the problem.

Especially difficult at these times is that other people are roped into the accusatory enterprise. Even our best friends can, in their attempt to make sense out of what is happening to us, fall in league with the enemy: "Where there's smoke, there's fire, Job; why don't you just fess up to it?" That (because none of us is sinless) can sound like a plausible reason for God's silence. And personal respon-sibility, of course, is usually the very reason for the messes we get into. Few of us are as righteous as Job.

So, what to do when God is silent?

1. Cover the possibility that you have grieved the Holy Spirit. This does not take long, and it takes the Lord only a few seconds or minutes to tell a truly listen-ing heart that it is guilty of sin. If you are guilty, con-fess. Tell the Lord you are bringing your sin under the blood of Jesus and tell yourself that He is now forgiving you, having paid for the right in the sacri-fice and resurrection of His Son.
2. If you are clear of any charges from the Lord, tell Him you believe that everything He does in relation to you is for your benefit, and that this silence will turn out for your blessing.
3. Turn every accusation over to the Lord for Him to deal with.
4. Actively believe that the length of this test of silence is under the careful scrutiny of the Lord, and that He will bring it to an end when it is best for you.

5. Keep doing your devotions, even if they are of no discernible benefit to you at all.
6. Go on going on.

Andrew Murray gave a wonderful example of how to respond to a time of testing when he wrote (quoted in *They Found the Secret*):

> First, He brought me here, it is by His will I am in this strait place: in that fact I will rest.
>
> Next, He will keep me here in His love, and give me grace to behave as His child.
>
> Then, He will make the trial a blessing, teaching me the lessons He intends me to learn, and working in me the grace He means to bestow.
>
> Last, in His good time He can bring me out again—how and when He knows.
>
> Let me say I am here,
> (1) By God's appointment,
> (2) In His keeping,
> (3) Under His training,
> (4) For His time.

That's faith!

3. Harassment

I have noticed that a couple times a year, in addition to the times before major events, the congregation comes under an attack of what I call harassment—the third flaming arrow of the evil one. This is a catch-all category for several kinds of mis-events. These things can be perfectly normal misfortune. But before accepting them, we should check to see whether they are sponsored by hell.

These harassments are designed to weaken our faith, induce us to let down our guard or to waver. As we hold up the shield of faith against them, they recede until they go away—that is, until the next go-round with the opposition. But the Lord will see to it that we get a season of rest before harassments are allowed to take place again.

Symptoms of Illness

I spoke of this earlier, but it is such a common attack that I will repeat myself. You might wake up with a runny nose. As soon as you become aware of the symptom, you usually think, "I'm going to be sick!" This combination of symptom-and-thought is a seed that the enemy is trying to plant in us. If we accept the seed, we tend to get sick. If we reject the seed—by rebuking the symptoms as well as the thought that we are going to be ill—the illness may leave (usually within a few hours) without getting any worse.

I just say out loud, "You symptoms of illness, I rebuke you in the name of Jesus. And you thoughts that I'm going to be sick, I rebuke you, too. Lord, make these things depart from me."

I experienced this routine seven times during the fall and winter months prior to writing these words. The first six times the symptoms left within hours. But the seventh time I was on vacation and did not rouse myself to sufficient resistance, with the result that I became sick.

Negative Thoughts

Sometimes we just get into a funk. The enemy can take advantage of this by piling up negative thoughts in our minds about ourselves or others. This is often the opening gambit for the onslaught of a depression (one that is more demonically inspired than the depression I combated with thanking in chapter 4).

These negative thoughts have to be rebuked. I often do this rebuking out loud: "You negative thoughts, I rebuke you. Get lost! I'm going to think about positive things."

Fatigue

Sometimes a harassing fatigue comes suddenly, descending on us just when we are supposed to do something for the Lord. "Oh, I'm just too tired to go to the meeting tonight!"

Rebuke fatigue. If it goes away, go to your meeting. If it stays, consider whether you have obeyed the Lord's command to rest.

Mechanical Things Breaking Down

Once, just prior to an important ministry trip to Australia, one of our team members, Donna, had three major kitchen appliances break down within thirty minutes. I cannot tell you how many times my cars have needed repair days before a ministry event. This is the annoying spite of an exasperated adversary.

What to do? Before things break down, ask for God's protection on them. After they break down, refuse to focus on the problem. Instead, stay focused on the Lord: "O Lord, the dumb old devil has picked on my car again. Please help me get it fixed, Lord. But I'm not going to let it deflect me from You or what You've got in store for me."

Miscommunication

For two weeks before I went to Argentina, my wife and I misunderstood almost everything the other said. I would mishear straightforward things she said; she would misinterpret the simplest things I said. It got to be laughable. Instead of getting ticked at each other, we recognized what was going on and refused to collaborate with the adversary by arguing with each other. Rather than try to sort out who made how much of a mistake, we quickly forgave each other for misspeaking or mis-hearing. (This is not the time to adjudicate percentages of guilt.)

Honestly, it got so bad we nearly resorted to hand signs. But it got no worse than the Lord thought would serve His purposes. Check?

Foibles of the Flesh

Do you tend to be irritable? Then check out provocations to irritability to see if they are from the enemy. Do you tend to be pessimistic, emotionally distant, late, oversensitive? These weaknesses can be pricked by the enemy to fan us into conflict with those around us.

God's answers to our foibles are the fruit of the Spirit, which counteract the fruit of the flesh. Let the Spirit's goodness counteract your pessimism; let His kindness counteract your coldness; let His self-control counteract your tendency to be late; let His joy counteract your oversensitivity. Counteraction is a dynamic by which God meets and resolves the foibles of the flesh.

4. Deception

The thrust of deception, the fourth flaming arrow of Satan, is to get the believer to abandon the biblical bases of his or her belief. Deception will appeal to common sense, to the latest study, to the dictates of reason, to the influence of famous people, to all manner of things. Deception says, "Look how unreasonable your position is." It tries to make you feel childish, unsophisticated, even absurd for believing as you do. Its real target is not you but the Word of God.

Is that not the very thing the snake said to Eve—"Did God really say . . . ?" (Genesis 3:1). Eve should have responded, "Yes, that's the very thing God said not to do, so take a walk! I'm not talking to you anymore."

Challenging and discrediting the Word of God is often the first stratagem of the enemy, for the Bible is the foundation for our beliefs. That does not mean that your interpretation of the Word will always be flawless; remember, it took the Holy Spirit to *write* Scripture and it takes the Holy Spirit to help us to *read* Scripture. But if you are determined to grow in your understanding and walk with the Lord, He will find portions of Scripture with which to guide and correct and encourage and heal and bless you.

If the enemy can cast doubt on God's Word, he can undermine the chief basis for God's dealings with you. Listen, the Lord counts His Word as terrifically important. It is not for nothing that the Son of God is called *the incarnate Word.* Nor do you have to understand everything in the Word in order to maintain intellectual integrity. You can say: "I don't understand all the ins and outs of the Word, and often I don't understand why the Word says what it does. But I'm not going to disbelieve or disobey it. Did Jesus rise from the dead? Yes, the Scriptures declare it plainly. How did He rise? I don't have to know that in order to believe it. I will continue to study and meditate and listen. If God wants me to comprehend more, I will grow into that comprehension. But I refuse to allow my level of comprehension to determine my level of belief."

5. The Attack on the Will

The will, as I have said, is the locus of belief. Let me reconstruct a graph I used earlier, with some additions.

In this graphic, the spirit and will are shaded to represent that Satan does not have direct access to them. The spirit, the most important part of a human being, can be impacted by Satan only through the will. It is the will that decides to sin. If I sin, I have a sick spirit as a result, which I experience as a guilty conscience.

Conscience is a role that the spirit performs. It tells me I have disobeyed God, broken fellowship with Him and am in need of reconciliation. If I ignore my conscience,

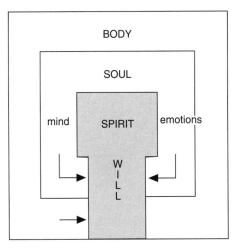

then the sickness in my spirit spreads to other aspects of my being: I can become physically sick, emotionally disturbed, mentally confused or relationally alienated.

So the spirit is Satan's real target. If he can get us to sin, he has usurped our core-level fellowship with our heavenly Father. If he can further impact us with dullness, rebellion and deception, he can do serious damage to our relationship with God and, consequently, our ministries against the kingdom of darkness.

But God has so constructed us that Satan can impact our spirit—which is in union with the Holy Spirit—only through our will. And he can affect our will only through our mind, emotions and body. Operationally, this means that Satan's main target is our will. This is the fifth fiery arrow that Satan launches against us.

The will, then, is the bastion against the influence of the enemy. It is in a protected place, directly inaccessible to its adversary and fueled by its contact with the spirit.

The function the will performs, as we have already seen, is that of *decision-making.* It receives input from the spirit, mind, emotions, body and world. When it decides for the

Lord, it is in the will of God. When it decides against the Lord, it is out of the will of God.

The word we use for this role is the word *faith*. God has constructed us so that faith operates exclusively in this faculty called the will. That is, *faith is a matter of making decisions.* This is why Billy Graham is said to have declared that "*decision* is the most important word in the English language." The decision to accept Christ Jesus into one's heart is a decision that has temporal and eternal ramifications that are past counting.

But the will does not simply make a once-for-all decision for Christ. The will is being assailed constantly by the enemy in order to induce it to change its decisions. If it changes its decisions, it changes its faith. It is constantly required, therefore, to protect, confirm, update and extend its decisions.

Satan knows that faith operates in the will. He also knows that he does not have direct access to the will. So he uses what he does have direct access to—the body, the mind and the emotions—to get at the will. Notice that I have drawn arrows aimed at the will from the mind, emotions and body, indicating the attacks that Satan can engineer. What Satan wants you to do is use your will to make a decision that lines up with *his* will instead of God's. He cannot make you make the decision, so he will try to get you to make his decision through the influence of what he can do to your body, mind or emotions.

I have spoken several times of Satan's use of the symptoms of illness and thoughts to induce us to accept a seed of illness. This is a prime example. What is his target? Our will. If he can get our will to agree with the symptoms and thoughts, he can plant the illness in us. If we utilize our will against the symptoms and thoughts, we can often reject the illness.

Does that mean my own body and mind and emotions are my enemy? No, no, no! Those elements of my being are the creation of God, not the devil. God loves them and has declared them (along with the rest of us) "very good" (Genesis 1:31). It is just that He never designed them to be the agents of faith. Faith is the function, rather, of the will. When the enemy uses my body and mind and emotions to get at my will, I am responsible to protect those parts of myself by using my will to reject the influence of the devil on them and to keep my will free from that influence.

Here's a comparison. I love my children to pieces. But each one of them has tried to manipulate me to make decisions that I consider improper. I still love them when they are pitching a fit, but I am not going to let that fit sway my decision. Likewise, I love my body, enjoy my mind and take great pleasure in expressing my emotions. But I do not intend to give any of these the right to make decisions in my life. They are not supposed to be the decider; my will is supposed to be the decider. So when the enemy tries to use my body, mind or emotions against me, I have to resist, accepting and cherishing them but refusing to use them instead of my will to decide.

Faith is an act of the will. Faith is making a decision.

Summary

Satan is canny. We make a great mistake if we underestimate his subtlety.

We make another mistake if we overestimate his power. While Satan has considerable power, he is no match for God, nor for the Son of God. His "match," if we have to use that term, is one of the archangels—Michael, for instance. And if we operate in the will and power of God, it is *Satan's* gates that won't stand *our* attack, rather than the reverse. It is he who is on the run, not we, unless we have fallen prey to his lies.

We have to fight Satan, but we need have nothing else to do with him.

7
Christian Misteaching

Teaching is one of the chief means God uses to inspire, instruct and correct our faith. Teaching is meant to help, not hinder us. Teaching is the most emphatic spiritual gift in which I personally operate. We teachers (bless our hearts!) often mean well and want nothing but good for those who learn from us. But we have to be careful that the teaching we bring is biblical, balanced, tested experientially and open to confirmation or correction from the wider Christian community. If not, we will lead people, including ourselves, amiss.

In conferences that I lead, the Holy Spirit often encourages me to pray for certain persons to be anointed with different gifts. When it comes to an anointing for teaching, I usually add an exhortation that goes something like this:

"This is a dangerous anointing. The Bible itself says, 'Not many of you should presume to be teachers, my brothers, because you know that we who teach will be judged more strictly' (James 3:1). Much of the trouble in the Church today is due to false teaching, for which God will judge teachers. Teachers are supposed to be listened to, so they must teach the truth. You teachers are to predigest the Word of God and then give it to His people in a manner in which they can take it in, as a mother bird predigests food for her chicks. You are to prove that the Word of God works. You must, therefore, live it out, putting your lives on the line in line with it. You must saturate your minds with it, ingesting large chunks of it for the rest of your life. Learn to think biblically, react biblically, evaluate biblically. Then give away what has been given to you."

At bottom, what is at stake in the matter of misteaching is heresy. That word may make you gasp—"Surely that's too strong a term!"—until we consider this definition of heresy: *Heresy is overdoing one truth at the expense of other truth.* Heresy is not a flat-out lie; it is a distortion of the truth.

The early and most insidious heresies had to do with the Persons of the Godhead, especially Jesus. Orthodoxy states that He was both man and God, but heresies emerged that compromised one or the other of these characteristics. Some said, "He was so God that He only appeared to be a man." This heresy expressed His divinity at the expense of His humanity. Others said, "He was the very best man who ever lived but He wasn't God." This heresy expressed His humanity at the expense of His divinity.

Modern heresies tend to overstate something about human beings. In the 1970s a charismatic heresy swept through the Church centering on the authority of pastors. This teaching gave pastors more authority in their people's lives than a balanced reading of Scripture permits. Pastors were telling people whom to marry, where to live, what kind of job to accept and the like. It proved disastrous to both congregations and individuals. I personally wept over the dissolution of some marriages that should never have occurred in the first place.

Today there are at least six misteachings going around

Hard Questions About Faith

Number Six: What's wrong and right about "name it and claim it"?

---

that influence the subject matter of this book: having faith. The first is the Word-faith movement.

1. Word-Faith

Word-faith adherents point to passages like this to back up their practice:

> "Have faith in God," Jesus answered. "I tell you the truth, if anyone says to this mountain, 'Go, throw yourself into the sea,' and does not doubt in his heart but believes that what he says will happen, it will be done for him."
>
> Mark 11:22–23

The Word-faith proponents would underline the word *says*. What you say is what you get.

What's Good About It

The truth of the Word-faith teaching is that uttering God-inspired words in faith has effect.

It is well demonstrated that words have power. I have led countless conferences in which one of the methods I have urged on those learning to minister healing is speaking to the condition of the sick person, commanding it to obey the Lord Jesus. Many, many persons have been healed through this practice. This is not the only way to get people healed, but it is one effective way when the situation calls for it.

The practice of thanking God for all things (Ephesians 5:20) is another example, as I have said, of the positive use of our words to release the power of God. Thanking God is such a powerful behavior that it actually changes our brain chemistry, which in turn influences our emotions toward well-being and optimism. Conversely, verbally ragging on ourselves also changes our brain chemistry so that our physical predilection is toward negative thoughts, which produce the emotion of depression.

Perhaps you have seen work associates talk themselves into being sick or losing a job or botching an opportunity because they voiced negative opinions about themselves, and thought that if they would just stop it, things could be different. Yes, there is power in our words. I cringe when I hear people speak damning words about our elected officials. Something of the power of the enemy is released against those officials, I believe, when citizens speak against them—which is, in effect, cursing them.

Verbal agreement with the Word of God can be astonishingly effective. I remember the blessing that came to me in a time of self-rejecting thoughts when I willfully agreed with 1 John 3:20: "If our heart condemn us, God is greater than our heart, and knoweth all things" (KJV).

"God," I said, "I decide to agree with Your Word, which encourages me to believe that You are greater than this heart of mine, which is condemning the bejabbers out of me."

I said that frequently. And after a while those condemning thoughts ceased.

At one time early in my current pastorate, I was distressed by criticism and disunity in our congregation. As a faith activity, I said Colossians 3:12–17 out loud over the empty sanctuary for thirty minutes every day for a week. At the end of that week, something clicked in my heart and I knew we would have few further problems with disunity, which has been the case.

These are some of the ways in which understanding the power of our words can be good.

What's Wrong with It?

I visited a very sick person in the hospital once who could not bring herself to say, "I'm sick," because it would be what these people call a "negative confession."

It was ludicrous. There she lay, evidencing the plainest data confirming her illness and frightened that God could not bear to hear her say those catastrophic words. I decided to tackle this blather head on.

"You're pretty *sick*, aren't you?"

She almost screamed in horror at my demonstration of a faithless negative confession.

"Are you worse for my having said it?" I asked gently.

She paused for about a minute. "No."

"Do you think God is wringing His hands in dismay over the fact that I, a mere mortal, have sapped all His divine strength by uttering those faithless syllables?"

"I guess not."

"Don't you realize you're not really trusting God with your illness because of your inability to admit you're sick? Your need to make a 'positive confession' is making you a liar—to God yet! Why don't you just plainly tell God right now that you're sick and that you'd like Him to help you?"

She did so—and she began to recover.

People can allow their theology to insinuate a chasm between them and God. The dishonesty that the Word-faith movement almost requires is itself far more detrimental to a healthy relationship with God than uttering honest words that acknowledge the situation as it actually is. God is the ultimate realist. He can face anything and is not afraid of anything, even a negative confessor.

Another of the chief faults of the Word-faith business is that it assumes the accuracy of self-diagnosis. Word-faith folk diagnose their problems naïvely and prescribe doses of Scripture equally naïvely to be administered to their needs. Some call this the application of scriptural promises: "Since I need money and God owns the cattle on a thousand hills—'Lord, sell off a couple of cows and send me the money.'"

But there is no *Why?* being asked about this need for money. One thing about God that He is not likely to abandon is His wisdom. We need to ask, "*Why* am I in need of money?"—for you can bet your last dollar there is a reason, and that God is very much on top of the situation.

George MacDonald gives us a clue in this brief statement: "When God can do what he will with a man, the man may do what he will with the world." We pounce our attention, of course, on the second phrase. But look at the first: "When God can do what he will with a man. . . ." When a person is so given over to the Person and purposes of God, when he has worked through the issues of rebellion and submission, when he is so in love with God that his greatest pleasure is to do His bidding, then God will give him extraordinary authority because He can trust him to use it appropriately.

Do you want to know if you are self-diagnosing accurately? Ask a believer who knows you well and has evidenced maturity. We do not see ourselves nearly as clearly as others do, and their input can save us from serious mistakes. Once we have gotten their input, we can listen to God for the faith-quickening Word He would like to speak into us.

The love of God is inexorable; it will keep seeking us and its will for us until it is satisfied. And it will not be thrown off-course by any amount of misunderstanding or misuse of the ways of faith. Am I saying that the believer has no authority before God? No, the believer has great God-given authority. But that authority can be mishandled so that the purposes of God are delayed. Remember, God has extraordinary respect for our free will.

Finding a Balance

I have said there is power in our words. I have said there is foolishness in being afraid to say something negative. Where is the balance point between these opposites? I think balance can be found in several factors.

First, what is your general or customary attitude? Do you habitually speak negatively? Is your speech filled with irony? Is there a bite in your humor? Then you might profitably determine to change your speech patterns to reflect a more hopeful, positive attitude. Your words do have power. What forces are you loosing by the way you use words? Do you think it is always foolishness to speak powerfully to conditions in the name of the Lord?

Second, what is your legalism quotient? "It is for freedom that Christ has set us free," Paul reminded the Galatians (5:1), so we must avoid letting legalism creep into our thinking and evaluating. Legalism takes the *good* out of the good news and replaces it with another form of bondage—religious bondage. Legalism is immaturity infused with zeal. And legalism, while masquerading as faith, is the opposite of faith because it establishes itself instead of faith as the substance of what is not seen. People end up having faith in their legalistic utterances rather than in the living God.

Balance comes with maturity. I cannot give you a ruler that you can hold up against religious practices to invariably judge them rightly. Balance comes from maturity and maturity is a process born of honesty, humility, teachability and experience that one has reflected on. The Pharisees refused to grow up in response to surprising words and actions from the Son of God. Their legalistic zeal put Him to death.

We do *not* yet see through a glass clearly. We make mistakes. The legalist denies that he is making a mistake in a false notion that to question a course of action is to evidence a lack of faith. In this misguided zeal, parents have killed ailing children by withholding crucial, God-given medicine from them. That is legalism run amok, bondage, the very thing that counters the cross of Christ.

In the final analysis we must put our faith in God. If we put our faith in religious practices, we make them gods. If we put our faith even in the Word of God, we make our comprehension of it god. God alone is God. We must put our faith in Him alone. He may choose to vindicate our religious practices or counter them or even ignore them. If our faith is in Him, whatever He does will benefit and mature us. But if our faith is in these lesser things, their failures will cast us adrift until we get our focus back on Him alone.

2. The Prosperity Teaching

It is surely the will of God that His people experience well-being. But a teaching that made the rounds in America a decade ago is now cutting a swath through Africa and causing enormous confusion and distress to the Body of Christ. It is a doctrine based on one or two verses that Christians have construed to mean that God wants everyone to enjoy economic prosperity, even wealth. If it seems a tad obnoxious to you that the richest nation on earth should export greed-based doctrines to destitute countries, you are on the right track.

Prosperity teaching tries to lock God into a money-dispensing machine that disgorges monetary blessings on those who know how to program it—i.e., have faith. It is a new form of an old heresy, Gnosticism. Gnostics (from the Greek word *gnosis*, knowledge) believe that special knowledge will get you goodies—salvation, problem-solving and the like. It appeals to intellectuals because it assumes a distinction between the bright and the not-so-bright. If you are mentally quick, or if you possess secret knowledge, you can expect your knowledge to deploy man's or God's power to your benefit.

At base, prosperity teaching appeals to the worst in man—pride. And spiritual pride is the worst sin of all. "I've got it made, so God must be on my side." That sentiment is loathsome to a biblical worldview. Pick up a concordance sometime and look through the passages on the poor. It will be clear that God does, in fact, draw a distinction between the rich and the poor; but it is the poor, not the rich, who have His special blessing.

The prosperity people take this verse and apply it to faith-grabbed riches: "Beloved, I pray that you may prosper in all things and be in health, just as your soul prospers" (3 John 2, NKJV). They assume that *prosper* means—what? Why, money, of course!

God is concerned with our financial condition. Over half of Jesus' parables concern money. And thousands of Christians all over the world have encouraging testimonies about how God has met financial needs. I myself could tell a dozen such stories from my own life.

But listen to James 4:3: "You ask and do not receive, because you ask amiss, that you may spend it on your pleasures" (NKJV). This passage is found just a few pages in the New Testament before the so-called prosperity passage. Even closer—and in the words of the same writer as the so-called prosperity passage—is this injunction: "But whoever has this world's goods, and sees his brother in need, and shuts up his heart from him, how does the love of God abide in him?" (1 John 3:17, NKJV). A balanced look at Scripture cannot justify greed masquerading as faith, no matter how faithful it sounds.

Prosperity teaching appeals to the greed that lies dormant in every human heart. It predisposes one to gain one's life for Jesus' sake rather than lose one's life for His sake. God enjoys giving His children material blessings. But I have found that those blessings usually come as a byproduct of a selfless work or attitude. It is like the time Jesus said, "Whoever wants to become great among you must be your servant, and whoever wants to be first must be your slave" (Matthew 20:26–27). It is O.K. to desire greatness, He is saying, but the only way to get there is through servitude to others. Greatness is a byproduct of serving others rather than a target toward which one can selfishly direct oneself.

Material blessings are like that. They come from the hand of a generous God who observes generosity in the believer and chooses to reward it. I have noticed that the one who gets blessed never expects it.

In 1980 I was offered a free ticket to a 21-day trip to Bavaria, Rome, the Holy Land and Athens if I would be a spiritual director of the tour group. When I asked the Lord if I could accept the offer, He replied, *Only if you take your wife.* Apparently He thought it was too important a trip to take alone.

When I inquired about the cost, however, I was told that a regular ticket cost $2,765. I gasped. There was no chance I could save up that much money in the nine months before the trip. Nevertheless, Sue and I began to put aside what money we could. In addition, we collected and turned in newspapers and aluminum cans.

Somehow, each time a payment was due, we met it. People began giving us gifts of cash and others gave me honoraria for leading seminars and retreats. A month before we were to go, we made the last payment. In fact, when I added up all the money that had come in, it came to $3,800, more than a thousand dollars beyond the price of the ticket!

I was flabbergasted. I walked into the church sanctuary and put the paperwork on the altar.

"Why have You done this?" I asked.

Immediately the Lord reminded me that the number of transients we had taken into our home to date was 38. *I gave you a hundred bucks apiece.*

"But, Lord," I protested, "that's not why we took them in."

I know, son, but I wanted to reward you anyway.

So we went on that glorious trip. The Lord prospered us. But it was a byproduct of other things, not something we could directly lay our hands on.

3. New Age

Doug Gregg, a partner of mine in other works, gives this definition of New Age:

> The New Age, holistic spirituality and human potential movements are forms of false religion which focus on untapped resources within the self and hold out the deceptive promise of wholeness. In reality they draw on occult sources of power, offering a counterfeit satisfaction of spiritual hunger and leaving people worse off than before.

Since his fall, Satan has always been a competitor with and copier of God. Is there such a thing as genuine guidance from God? The Scriptures clearly indicate that there is. So what does Satan do? He produces a counterfeit copy of the genuine article. He has been doing this for centuries. At present, so-called "New Age" practices—which are really an invasion into Western civilization of Hinduism—are one of the bogus spiritualities he is pushing.

The thing that is really sad is that some who call themselves Christians are experimenting with these forms of spirituality. You do not have to look hard to find various blends of Christianity and New Age. The Bible calls these things "doctrines of demons" (1 Timothy 4:1, NKJV) and "detestable practices" (Deuteronomy 18:12), warning us in the strongest language to have nothing to do with them and predicting dire consequences for those who perpetrate them:

> There were also false prophets among the people, just as there will be false teachers among you. They will secretly introduce destructive heresies, even denying the sovereign Lord who bought them.... These teachers will exploit you with stories they have made up.
>
> 2 Peter 2:1, 3

> They are godless men, who change the grace of our God into a license for immorality and deny Jesus Christ our only Sovereign and Lord. . . . These men speak abusively against whatever they do not understand; and what things they do understand by instinct, like unreasoning animals—these are the very things that destroy them.... They are clouds without rain, blown along by the wind; autumn trees, without fruit and uprooted—twice dead.
>
> Jude 4, 10, 12

Part of the reason for the rise of New Age practices in the West is the anemia of Western Christianity, which has failed to display the Spirit's power. How many of us can say to our converts what Paul said to his:

> My message and my preaching were not with wise and persuasive words, but with a demonstration of the Spirit's power, so that your faith might not rest on men's wisdom, but on God's power.
>
> 1 Corinthians 2:4–5

By default, insipid Christianity invites seekers to look elsewhere, and Satan is always ready with a clever copy of the real thing. This is not a book on demonstrations of the Spirit's power—miracles, healings, power encounters, spiritual battles, deliverance from demonization, emotional healings and the gifts of the Holy Spirit. But let me assure you, these things are still going on wherever Christianity is virile. Where it is anemic, insipid and flaccid, on the other hand, Christianity leaves itself open to invasion.

Read Deuteronomy 18:9–13 in several translations. There you will find God commanding His people to have nothing to do with

> Child sacrifice (abortion?)
> Divination (palm-reading, water-witching, tarot cards)
> Astrology
> Hypnotism
> Sorcery (casting spells, using incantations such as the
>   Hindu *ohm*)
> Spiritual curses
> Séances
> Channeling
> Using spiritists
> Visualizing outside scriptural inspiration

These activities are forbidden because Satan is their author and we are to have no collusion with him. But because Satan is their author, they work. I want to warn you that some reasonable-sounding behavior will be presented to you as something with which to experiment. Hold this thing up alongside Scripture and see how it fares. If Scripture warns against it, have nothing to do with it, no matter how reasonable it sounds. It is a deception. It will poison you.

4. Being Divided by Doctrines

St. Paul had a lot to say about doctrine, but he never misunderstood the role of doctrine in the Church. "Love never fails," he said, not, "Doctrine never fails."

May I define a couple of key words? *Dogma* is what all Christians everywhere believe. Dogma is what is summarized in the Apostles' and Nicene Creeds. Dogma speaks about the Trinity, the incarnation, salvation, heaven and hell, the Church as the Body of Christ and basic beliefs.

Doctrine is the word given to sub-compartments of dogma. It is at the level of doctrine that Christians find themselves believing quite different things. Doctrines speak, for example, of church government, the lesser sacraments, religious practices and eschatology (when and how the end of the age will occur).

For many decades Christians have vilified each other for these doctrinal views. We have waged arguments as though these matters were at the top of God's agenda, when His Word declares that *unity*, not ideological conformity, is His agenda. How many jokes have you heard about different denominations and how they interact in heaven?

I am part of a group of pastors in my town who pray together each Tuesday morning. One of these brothers has a close associate in his denomination who has ridiculed me in books for doctrinal positions I have taken. I could choose to argue, and I hope I could debate these issues fairly well. But it is more important to God for me to be one with my brother in the group of pastors than to be victorious over his associate. So we refuse to debate these things. In view of the need of the world for the grace of God, these doctrines are insignificant. I refuse to let them divide me from my brother. And I have forgiven and continue to pray for his associate who wrote about me.

Our pastors' prayer fellowship has discovered that it will take the whole Church in the San Fernando Valley to impact the whole Valley for Christ. What's more, we have learned that God has a peculiar role for each congregation to play in His plan for our area. Our own congregation, for example, seems to be pretty good at training people for hands-on ministries to the sick and poor. We are lousy at developing strong programs for enhancing family life. But guess what? We have found that another congregation in town excels at this very thing. What are we to do? Learn from them how to bless families? Maybe. But I suspect we are to ask them if our families can come to their programs and benefit from them.

In His tremendous mercy and creativity, the Lord also brought me into a close working relationship with members of a key West Coast Adventist congregation through Gary and Cyndee, two of their leaders. Every once in a while I kind of wonder about some Adventist practices— being vegetarians, for instance, or worshiping on Saturdays. But we have been so busy being the people of God and spreading His Kingdom that we have not bothered to take the time to explain our doctrines to each other. These are dear, dear brothers and sisters in Jesus. I love and admire them greatly. I respect them and their doctrinal positions, and they respect mine. But we do not have to understand each other doctrinally in order to work together for the Kingdom.

5. Sexual Idolatry

Many of the historic mainline denominations today are particularly vulnerable to a well-known sociological dynamic in which vigor gradually gives way to dilution, which ends in mediocrity. In that third stage, mediocrity, either renewal occurs and vigor is recovered or else further deterioration occurs. Much renewal is going on in these denominations, thank God, but there is also much continued mediocrity and downgrading of authentic Christianity.

Chief among the departures from the faith is sexual idolatry. Compromise with secular positions on sexuality is not a doctrine-level but a dogma-level concern, for it erodes the most fundamental matter—the worship of God. God intends His people to experience intimacy with Himself. The very word in Greek that is translated *worship* literally means to approach to kiss. Worship is meant to include close, personal, affectionate expressions between God and His people. Worship means esteeming God. When we esteem something *other* than God, we engage in idolatry.

When the devil tempted Adam and Eve to eat the fruit of the tree of the knowledge of good and evil, what was his target? Well, what did Adam and Eve cover when they became aware they had sinned? Not their eyes, with which they had seen the fruit. Not their hands, with which they had seized it. Not their mouths, with which they had eaten it. They covered their genitals. Satan's target was their sexuality, for it is sexuality that is intended by God to express true worship; and it is sexuality that is meant by Satan to express idolatry.

Vertical intimacy with God is woven into a lateral intimacy between husband and wife, which is the sign of that vertical oneness. Why do you think the Church is called the Bride of Christ? Sexual oneness in marriage is the nearest sign to human beings of the quality of relationship God wants with us. When one compromises that standard by experiencing sex outside of wedlock, one collaborates with Satan's rather than God's goals for sexuality and worship. Sexuality becomes idolatrous.

It is not for nothing that the chief satanic mechanism to pollute the people of God in the Old Testament was the enticement to worship fertility goddesses. How did one

worship them? By having intercourse with cult prosti-
tutes, either male or female. On one occasion God acted
with strong retribution, killing 23,000 Israelites to demonstrate the utter seriousness of sexual sin. (Those who wish
to pursue this matter are strongly encouraged to read *Eros
Redeemed* by John White.)

Compassionate-sounding, reasonable, research-veri-
fied positions in opposition to the teachings of Scripture
on sexuality are being presented in every mainline
denomination. Although they appear progressive and
helpful, these positions are unraveling the very fabric of
the faith and subjecting the entire Church to judgment.
They must be resisted, not by endless debates but by righteous living and by prayer. Only righteousness can display
the genuine item for those with eyes to see. Only prayer
can defeat these Christian sexual heresies.

A certain reserve inhibits me from sharing several stories in which greatly outnumbered prayer warriors defeated heretical votes in denominational parliamentary
settings. Let the reader simply be encouraged to link up
with mature believers who will teach him how to release
the unlimited power of God into those settings. The arm
of the Lord is never short when His people place His hand
on their concerns.

6. Liberation Theology

Those who promote what is called liberation theology
rightly identify social ills that need correction. But
although the diagnosis is accurate, the prescription veers
strongly from God's agenda when terrorism ends up as
the recommended behavior. I think these theologians
incorrectly ignore the power of obedience to civil authority. When you obey civil authority, as Paul enjoined in
Romans 13, God takes it upon Himself to clean up that
civil authority.

Does that mean civil authority is never in the wrong, never to be resisted? No. But the means of resistance is not fighting fire with fire, which just gets everybody burned. Biblical resistance is obeying God rather than men (Acts 5:29) *and* being willing to suffer retribution from the authority, blessing those who persecute you, praying for those who abuse you and tolerating their punitive measures.

Summary

In this age of image consciousness, manipulating public consciousness and careful self-positioning, we need to be aware that merely to call a teaching "Christian" does not propel it into agreement with God. As the Bible itself declares, the Spirit and the Word—both in agreement—are the guides to what is true and false. And always remember, understanding follows (not precedes) obedience.

Now let's look at what doubt really is.

8

False Notions About Doubt

Once Jesus took a shortcut across a corner of the Sea of Galilee, which necessitated His walking for a bit on water. This happened to bring Him close to the disciples in their boats, who were terrified by the sight, thinking they were seeing a ghost. Jesus reassured them, at which point Peter said, "If it's really You, tell me to come to You on the water." When Jesus beckoned to Peter to get out of the boat and walk toward Him, Peter did a very human thing: He had second thoughts about what he was doing and he began to sink.

For a moment Peter modeled for us how to do the impossible: Keep your eyes on Jesus. Then he modeled taking one's eyes *off* Jesus, consequently being no longer up to the impossible. Jesus did not comment on the successful part of Peter's experience, but on the failure: "Why did you doubt?" (Matthew 14:31).

Doubt is a tough nut to crack. It is so important that I have decided to spend a whole chapter on it. As usual, it occurs to me to look at the word that is translated doubt. It is *distazo*—a very interesting word. Literally it means split-standing. Thus, it makes perfect sense to recall Peter standing on the surface of the water. Because he stood divided, he failed to carry through on what Jesus had beckoned him to accomplish. One foot stood on the command of Jesus to come, but the other foot stood on the human impossibility of doing such a thing. Gasp! Splash! Rebuke! What an ignominious sequence.

The letter of James deals with "split-standedness," using the idea of double-mindedness:

> If any of you lacks wisdom, he should ask God, who gives generously to all without finding fault, and it will be given to him. But when he asks, he must believe and not doubt, because he who doubts is like a wave of the sea, blown and tossed by the wind. That man should not think he will receive anything from the Lord; he is a double-minded man, unstable in all he does.
>
> James 1:5–8

This passage offers great encouragement—and a warning. God "gives generously to all without finding fault." Hooray! This encourages us to ask boldly, for "it will be given to [us]." God is pleased, as we saw in chapter 1, when He is able to give to His children. But there is a catch, isn't there? "He must believe and not doubt." And if the person who asks is blown about like the waves, he or she is described as double-minded, unstable.

I like James. He is a straight-shooter and will tell you exactly where you stand. He is making two points here about faith. First, what is the opposite of double-minded? Why, single-minded, of course. James is saying that we have to make up our minds about our requests to God.

Do you really want what you are asking for? Are you as persuaded as you can be that it is the thing you should be seeking? Some people are too quick to ask; they ask without thinking out the ramifications of their request. Others do not know their own hearts. I find I am often in this predicament. I do not really know what I want. One day I feel like this, the next day I feel like that. I am exactly what James describes as being blown and tossed by the wind.

When we are in that state, the best thing to ask for is guidance from God, for He knows what we should be asking for.

This can take quite a bit of time. At the time I am writing this book, I have been questioning God for more than a year about something related to my career, and still I do not know what to ask for. So I am waiting, asking for guidance. I am not yet at the point of asking for something in particular because I do not yet know what to ask for.

The second point James is making is that double-mindedness equals instability. I was pondering this once when the picture came to my imagination of a fellow getting into a boat from a dock. With one foot on the dock and the other in the boat, he was balanced so precariously that it was apparent no one had better try to hand him anything!

When God withholds from the unstable, it is an act of mercy, for to grant them their request would be to tip them even more off-balance. That is why "that man should not think he will receive anything from the Lord."

Now be honest in response to this question: Do you identify more with Peter walking on the water or Peter sinking under the water? If the latter, do you see why Jesus focused on the failure? This is the experience of the vast majority of people, and it need not be. It was not Peter's *feelings* but his *behavior* that Jesus rebuked.

Which leads us to the first point.

Doubt Is Not a Feeling

You know, it just might be worth the price of this book to get this one point: *Doubt is not how you feel.*

Everybody you can think of in the Bible experienced feelings of doubt, including Jesus. Thank God! Emotions are like colors. How bland life would be if there were only black and white! Sometimes our emotions are pleasant, sometimes painful, but what an astonishing deficit we would have if we did not experience them, even the painful ones. "Feeling good" has become almost a god in our age, and we do all manner of dysfunctional things to try to feel good.

I understand. I want to feel good, too. But feeling good is like what the philosophers in the golden age of Greece said about happiness: You cannot directly attain it, for it is the byproduct of other things, just as material blessings are usually the byproduct of a selfless work or attitude (as we saw in the last chapter). The U.S. Constitution may be a touch misleading when it guarantees everyone the right to pursue happiness, implying that you *can* pursue it. But feeling good is the result of other behaviors; it happens somewhere en route the long way 'round.

"Does God want us to feel good?"

Of course!

"Then how come we can't just directly grab onto good feelings?"

Because it doesn't work that way.

"Why not?"

I don't fully know.

I hope that little exchange does not cast you into despair. I also hope you do not simply reject it—because it is true. I do not know why good feelings cannot be attained directly. But I know that they cannot. And that is the very reason faith has little to do with feelings, either positive or negative.

God wants us, in cooperation with His Lordship, to be in control of our lives. But we are not in control of our feelings. (We have talked about this at some length already.) Have you struggled with depression, as I have? If so, then you will know what I mean. If we could just decide not to feel depressed, it would be grand, but that is not how it works. Getting out of depression occurs as a byproduct of doing other things, some of which we have discussed already—things like thanking God, rebuking the enemy, getting inner healing, correcting immoral behavior, forgiving those who have offended us, refusing to engage in counterproductive relationships. But you cannot get out of depression just by saying you are no longer going to be depressed.

So what are we in control of? Our will. Just as faith is a decision, *doubt is also a decision,* an act of the will. One *chooses* to doubt. All manner of stimuli external to the will can influence the will—feelings, circumstances, "evidences"—but doubt is purely an act of the will.

When Jesus, who had just scared the dickens out of the disciples, said to them, "Fear not," He was speaking not to their emotions but to their wills, which were in danger of being swayed by their emotions. We are not in control of our emotions, but we do not have to let those emotions stampede our wills, forcing us to act in accordance with our feelings.

The Elastic Clause of Unbelief

The elastic clause of unbelief covers a wide spectrum of situations. It runs something like this: "I don't know why this isn't going to work, but it isn't." I have been astounded by how many people, myself included, have exercised the elastic clause of unbelief. When we do, we are allowing other factors—feelings, circumstances, opinions—to override our wills.

Remember, the will is the target of both God and Satan. It is your decider that they are trying to influence.

The general sense that things will not turn out all right veers perilously close to sin. The worry that Jesus spoke

> ### Hard Questions About Faith
>
> *Number Seven: Why does faith seem to come more easily for some, while others wrestle or are more naturally skeptical? Is this credited to the spiritual ones or held against the "skeptics"?*

about in the Sermon on the Mount *is* sin, for it assumes that God is unable and/or uninterested to care for us.

Now, I know that some of you are temperamentally prone to worry and that you have been created that way. Just for fun, let's look at two temperamental factors from the Myers-Briggs Temperament theory:

Judging Attitude	Perceiving Attitude
Settled	Pending
Decided	Gathering more data
Fixed	Flexible
Planning ahead	Adapting as you go
Running your life	Letting life happen
Looking for closure	Open to options
Decision-making	Treasure-hunting
Planned	Open-ended
Completed	Emerging
Decisive	Tentative
Wrapping it up	Something will turn up
Urgent	There's plenty of time
Deadline!	What deadline?
Get this show on the road	Let's wait and see

Which of these attitudes do you think has a greater tendency to worry? The judging attitude, of course. Those who possess this attitude are called J's in the Myers-Briggs lingo. J's tend to be pessimistic, careful, better-put-something-aside-for-a-rainy-day sort of people. God bless 'em, they are the cornerstone of society. I am one of them myself. Without them the rest of humanity would be scatter-brained and fickle. But J's tend almost unconsciously to practice the elastic clause of unbelief. It is something they should be on the alert for, or they will lapse into negative faith.

Those of you who are J's, let me encourage you to monitor your thoughts and emotions to be on the lookout for negative thinking and feeling. Counteract these tendencies with willfully optimistic attitudes and actions toward God.

Honest and Dishonest Doubt

There are times when one must simply deal with doubt. We can deal with doubt honestly or dishonestly.

The apostle Thomas is a good example of the honest doubter. It is clear that he wanted to believe with all his heart but just could not permit himself to do so without evidence. Jesus did not commend Thomas for his doubt but He did answer it: "Put your finger here; see my hands. Reach out your hand and put it into my side. Stop doubting and believe" (John 20:27).

This was agonized doubt—doubt that wanted to believe. God may not like doubt but He will deal mercifully and generously with it.

Dishonest doubt is doubt that has no intention of believing, no matter how much evidence is produced.

You cannot fool God; He knows which kind you intend.

Then some of the Pharisees and teachers of the law said to him, "Teacher, we want to see a miraculous sign from you." He answered, "A wicked and adulterous generation asks for a miraculous sign! But none will be given it except the sign of the prophet Jonah."

Matthew 12:38–39

These people had seen or talked to plenty of witnesses who had seen miracles, but still they refused to believe.

Hard Questions About Faith

Number Eight: Shouldn't I infer, according to Hebrews 11:6 and Jesus' constant rebuking of the disciples, that God is displeased with me if I don't have enough faith?

Nor would they believe when they had evidence of the Jonah-like entombment and release with which Jesus predicted His death and resurrection.

"Woe to you, Korazin! Woe to you, Bethsaida! If the miracles that were performed in you had been performed in Tyre and Sidon, they would have repented long ago in sackcloth and ashes."

Matthew 11:21

If one seeks evidence in order to *release* belief, he will probably find it. If one seeks evidence to *compel* belief, he will probably not find enough. He will be guilty of trifling with God, of judging God rather than being judged by God, of trying to compel God to come to him on his terms rather than going to God on His terms.

The Pharisees were guilty of dishonest doubt. They were playing a game. They were insincere. Jesus condemned them.

The Assault of Doubt

I want to begin this section by reminding you that I am postulating a captaincy of the human being that resides in the spirit. The spirit is the captain, the will is its executive officer, and the mind and emotions lieutenants in charge of mental and emotional data.

Romans 8 and Galatians 5 deal extensively with this matter of supremacy. Paul states the case clearly in these verses:

> Those who live according to the sinful nature have their minds set on what that nature desires; but those who live in accordance with the Spirit have their minds set on what the Spirit desires. The mind of sinful man is death, but the mind controlled by the Spirit is life and peace; the sinful mind is hostile to God. It does not submit to God's law, nor can it do so. Those controlled by the sinful nature cannot please God. You, however, are controlled not by the sinful nature but by the Spirit, if the Spirit of God lives in you.
>
> Romans 8:5–9

Thus we see in the Scriptures that it is neither the flesh nor the soul but the spirit that must be in charge.

If the *mind* ruled, it would have to *understand* the directives it was being given. It is the nature of the mind to seek to understand, and not to give itself to what it does not yet understand. So if the mind were to exercise its presidency dependably, the things of the faith would have to be logical. The problem with an intellectual presidency is that the intellect is a finite tool with which to grasp *infinite* reality. If I can believe or cooperate only with what I understand, then I have exempted myself from participating in huge segments of the spectrum of reality, for most of it lies beyond my comprehension.

If the *emotions* ruled, they would have to *feel* good about the directives they were being given in order to agree with integrity. The problem with this, as I have stated, is that I am not in direct, manipulable control of my emotions. Many other factors have more influence over my emotions than I do. I am powerless to tell an emotion to stop being what it is and become something else. An emotion is defiant, going right on being what it is no matter what I tell it. So if I am to exercise any responsibility for my actions, emotions are the loose cannon on deck, for they are unpredictable and uncontrollable.

It is the *will* (as I have been postulating throughout this book) to which Jesus addresses His directions. The will is in a different category from the mind and the emotions. I have tried to represent this difference in the graph I have been using (which I use again later in this chapter). Notice that the section delineating the will begins in the spirit and extends through the whole of the person—spirit, soul and body. By this I mean to indicate that the will carries a breadth of extent and access untrue of the mind and emotions.

The will has an obvious advantage over the mind: Something need not surrender to the laws of logic in order to be believed. Nor does the will have to feel good about the thing it is being asked to believe. All the will needs in order to take faithful action is the conviction that what it is being told is the immediate will of God. The will does not have to *think* something is a good idea. It does not have to *feel* positive about it. It has only to *decide* in order to exercise effective faith. It is as simple—and challenging!—as that.

Jesus could have produced all manner of reasons that would have excused Him from the necessity of the cross. It is clear that He felt ghastly horror at the prospect of going to the cross. In such cases, it is the will that saves one, even when that one is the Son of God. Remember what He said, three times yet: "Nevertheless not my will, but thine, be done" (Luke 22:42, KJV). Only the will can say that. Only the will can act in opposition to itself or to the mind or to the emotions. For the will originates in the spirit.

Are the mind and emotions enemies, then? No. They were both created by God. When they are sanctified, their roles are (as we will see later in this chapter) irreplaceably good. Their function is not decision-making, however, but providing information. The mind and emotions may be lieutenants, but the captain is the one responsible for exercising authority. This captain, the spirit, exercises his authority through his executive officer, the will. The will is superior in rank to the mind and emotions but inferior to the spirit. The will is the avenue of access that the spirit has with the mind and emotions and body.

Recall what we said in chapter 6: Some parts of the human being are directly accessible to the devil and some are not. Remember that I shaded the spirit and the will to indicate that Satan does not have direct access to them. In other words, Satan can directly touch your body; he can directly influence your thoughts; he can directly impact your emotions. But he cannot directly touch your spirit or your will. Consequently, if he is going to influence them, he must do so indirectly, through the other factors.

How Doubt Attacks Faith

Since our bodies, minds and emotions are the only factors in us directly manipulable by Satan, these are what he uses to pressure our wills into making unfaithful decisions. Characteristically it works something like this:

Will: "I confess my sins to You, Lord, and ask You to forgive them."

Mind: "You don't really believe He forgives you, do you? You're too sinful, and besides, you're not sorry enough."

Emotion: [A sinking *flip-flop* in the stomach that seems to verify what the mind just said.]

Will: "Oh, gosh, maybe I'm *not* forgiven. I surely haven't fallen down weeping over my sins."

Mind: "Actually, it isn't your fault. You don't want to *fake* repentance. It's just not time for true repentance."

Emotion: [A kind of lifting at the idea of not having to weep its guts out.]

Will: "Yeah, I guess so. If I'm not ready, I'm not ready. I'll probably be forgiven later. . . ."

What happened here first is that the will made a faithful decision. But that decision was attacked through the mind and emotions. Then the will changed its decision, agreeing with the mind and emotions rather than with the Word of God, which declares, "If we confess our sins, he is faithful and just and will forgive us our sins and purify us from all unrighteousness" (1 John 1:9). The person went away unforgiven because his faith was neutralized.

Notice that 1 John does not say, "If we fall down on the floor sobbing and weeping for our sins for at least twenty minutes, then God may graciously deign to forgive us." No, it is cut-and-dried. Sincerity is not emotion, after all; it is decision. One may or may not feel something in the exercise of faith, but the faith itself is willful, not emotional. Emotions are incidental to faith.

Let's redo the scenario:

Will: "I confess my sins to You, Lord, and ask You to forgive them."

Mind: "You don't really believe He forgives you, do you? You're too sinful, and besides, you're not sorry enough."

Emotion: [A sinking *flip-flop* in the stomach that seems to verify what the mind just said.]

Will: "Did You notice that attack, Lord? Well, I decide

that You have forgiven me no matter what my mind and emotions tell me, for Your Word states that if I confess, I'm forgiven. Thank You, Jesus, for forgiving my sins."

If the will persists in making decisions in line with the Word and will of God, a lovely metamorphosis occurs in the mind and emotions. They begin to agree with the will.

The Fact-Faith-Feeling Train

Bill Bright of Campus Crusade for Christ draws a little picture of a simple train on the back of a tract :

The power is in the engine, the fuel is in the tender and the payload is in the caboose. Many people stand at the back of the tender, shoveling coal furiously into the caboose, which cannot convert it into energy.

If we invest faith in our feelings, we are expending energy uselessly—and we are looking backward as well. It is only when we shovel fuel into the engine that we get anywhere.

At first it may seem unappealing to have to place your faith in the cold fact of God's will, but that is what gets you chugging down the track of life. And because He loves you, guess what? *Feelings follow faith.* If you decide you are forgiven, you will soon feel forgiven, too. And if you decide you are forgiven, your thoughts will fall into line behind that decision and affirm it in due course, because your mind is being renewed.

I can imagine your next question: How long is "soon" and "in due course"? As soon as your decision is settled, tested and still settled. That may take a few minutes or a few days, depending on the strength of your decision. In major, contested areas of your life, it might take weeks or months. Remember that we likened faith to a muscle, which grows strong by being resisted. Every time you exercise your faith in opposition to your thoughts and feelings, it grows stronger. When God determines that it is strong enough, He allows the mind and emotions to support it.

The following poem from a devotional book sums up the point of the train image by stating it in reverse:

> Three men were walking on a wall,
> Feeling, Faith and Fact,
> When Feeling got an awful fall,
> And Faith was taken back.
> So close was Faith to Feeling,
> He stumbled and fell, too,
> But Fact remained,
> And pulled Faith back,
> And Faith brought Feeling, too.
>
> Mrs. Charles E. Cowman
> *Streams in the Desert,* vol. 2

The Anyway Factor

Genuine faith does not eradicate doubt. It acts *anyway* in the presence of doubt. Watchman Nee, in *What Shall This Man Do?* gives us a delightful look into this.

I love to recall the prayer of the early church for Peter's deliverance from the hands of wicked men. When Peter came back from the prison and knocked at the door where the church was in prayer, the believers exclaimed, "It is his angel." Do you see? There was faith there, true faith, the kind of faith that could bring an answer from God; and yet the weakness of man was still present, and doubt lurked just around the corner, as it were. But to-day the faith many of God's people claim to exercise is greater than that exercised by the believers gathered in the house of Mary the mother of John Mark. And they are so positive about it! . . .

These people are too credulous, too cock-sure. Their faith is not necessarily the genuine article. Even in the most devoted Christian, the earthen vessel is always there, and, at least to himself, it is always in evidence, though the determining factor is never the vessel but the treasure within. In the life of a normal Christian, just when faith rises positively to lay hold of God, a question may simultaneously arise as to whether perhaps he might be mistaken.

We are going to look further at the "earthen vessel" in chapter 12. For the moment let's simply realize that it is simplistic, even triumphalistic, to suppose that doubt will scamper away at the mere faithful decision of the will. Reality is more paradoxical than that. Opposites in the real world mix freely. One might even say that it is impossible to express real faith in the absence of doubt, for doubt is one of the prime testers of the muscle of faith.

The person who claims to be absolutely certain God is telling him or her to do something is probably self-deluded or dishonest. That kind of person is probably putting blind faith in his faith. "If I just believe hard enough," he might think subconsciously, "it'll work." But God, not faith, is what we are to have faith in.

It seems to please God to so monitor the details of our lives that the opportunity to exercise faith rarely occurs in the *absence* of facts and possibilities and feelings that can engender doubt. It is not a case of either faith or doubt. It is faith in the presence of doubt that pleases Him and enables Him to act on our behalf.

Positive Doubt

Is doubt always a bad thing? I don't think so. There is a positive role doubt can play. Mike Phillips comments,

> Doubt—even unbelief—can be a tool in God's hand, wielded, in the lives of those who allow it, for the *strengthening*, not the destruction, of faith.

Doubts, says MacDonald,

> are the messengers of the Living One to the honest. They are the first knock at our door of things that are not yet, but have to be understood. . . . Doubt must precede every deeper assurance; for uncertainties are what we first see when we look into a region hitherto unknown, unexplored, unannexed.

If you stop and think about it, I'll bet you have had this experience.

The first time I heard someone claim to have been healed through prayer, my response was to doubt it. But as more stories began to pour in from people I had no reason to suspect, my attitude gradually changed from "I doubt it!" to "Hmm . . ." to "Well, let me look into this" to "I believe now that this happens" to "O God, please heal Mark" to "Wow, did you see that wrist change?"

Sanctified Thinking and Emotions

In the face of my statement that doubt is a function of the will, one might think I am advocating a cold, bloodless, mechanical faith. I am not, of course. And please do not think I am saying that effective faith squelches either the mind or the emotions. God created intellect *and* emotion (as I have said before), so why would He care to squelch them?

In saying that faith is a matter of the will, I am saying that the will makes the final decision. At the same time, it is a fool to ignore the input of the mind and emotions.

Thinking

Just because the mind can be influenced by Satan does not mean it is totally untrustworthy. The Bible speaks strongly about being renewed in the spirit of your mind,

---

Hard Questions About Faith

Number Nine: How can I know what God is doing or wants to do in the invisible realm?

---

about guarding your mind, about not letting your thinking become darkened, about putting on the mind of Christ. The mind is a rightful advisor, and not just the advisee, of the will.

A mind filled with scriptural truth, submitted to the Lordship of Christ, alive with wonder at the majesty of God—this is a mind that can play a crucial role in advising the will. Because much truth is *trans*rational does not mean it is *anti*rational. The mind can provide godly reasons for the assent of the will to a certain course of action. Saturated with Scripture, it can provide quick warning when an ungodly course is being contemplated. Sanctified reason is an invaluable ally in the business of having faith.

The problem in our culture today, as I have suggested, is unsanctified reason—arrogant reason, uninformed reason, unsubmissive reason. "As he thinks in his heart, so is he," the Bible asserts (Proverbs 23:7, NKJV). This correlates with modern observations that thinking is the most potent of influences upon one's emotions, while emotions are strong stimulants to action. We now know that our mental self-talk streaks along at over 1,200 words per minute. If we allow our self-talk to run ungoverned under the influence of culture, rationality, accusation and deception, it will produce in us the kinds of emotions that will throw up hurdles to maturity, balance, health and fruitful endeavor for the Lord. If we bring our intellect into submission to the Lord, to His Spirit-revealed Word, to the foremanship of the will, then we are nurturing sanctified reason.

Emotions

Emotions, too, can provide invaluable input to the will. Often the stirrings of one's spirit are difficult to distinguish from the feelings they generate. We nearly always experience unpeace or an uncomfortable conscience in some measure as feelings. It might help to say that feelings lie on the surface while the spirit sits at the base of those feelings and is their source. Also, as I have just indicated, our thinking is a powerful stimulant to our emotions.

Let me drag up that old graphic again, with a few amendments.

Remember, the spirit is the receiver to which the Lord beams His signals. This input has to be transmitted to other faculties in the person so that it can be made use of. In the diagram, this influence is represented by the arrows originating in the spirit.

To a mentally oriented person, the impressions tend to be mostly mental. The little box on the line between spirit and mind indicates a window. If I know that window is there and learn how to open it, the Holy Spirit can get information through that window from my spirit to my mind. These take the form of quick impressions, pictures,

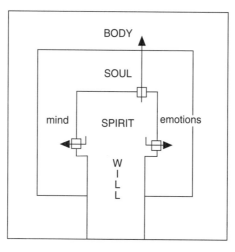

concepts, words and memories. The Scriptures call them "words of knowledge" and "words of wisdom."

For someone more emotionally oriented, the arrow may run from the spirit to the emotions. Such persons often experience sudden, even strong, surges of emotion, which they come to recognize as being from God. These, too, are words of knowledge or wisdom. One effective healer came to realize that when she felt a rush of compassion for a person, that person almost always got healed after being prayed for. We have quite a few persons in our congregation, generally women, who experience sudden risings of tears during prayer. They felt sheepish about it until they recognized the Holy Spirit as the Source of those tears, and that those tears almost always result in an effective release of God's power into the person or need or situation they are praying for.

What makes the difference between sanctified and unsanctified emotions? I wish I knew a nice, simple formula that you could enact in the next few minutes. It does not work that way. Because emotions are involuntary—beyond our conscious control—they are trustworthy indicators of our inner state. When we feel bad, something is wrong. But most of us make a great mistake when we assume that bad feelings are an accurate indication of the action we need to take to change them. Negative feelings tell us something is wrong; they do *not* tell us what to do about it.

Sanctified emotions come as a result of a host of other factors: knowing, believing and acting on the Word of God; cultivating intimacy with God; learning how to respond to spiritual warfare; engaging in mental and relational disciplines; growing in mutuality with other believers; seeking healing for damaged emotions. These factors will produce general health in one's emotional life. Even then, emotional input to the will must be evaluated before becoming the basis for willful action.

Some people even experience physical indicators from God (as indicated by the arrow to the body) that guide their prayers. Such people might feel a sudden pain someplace that, if they think about it, is abnormal for them. Then comes the realization that they are carrying (as it were) someone else's pain as an indication that God wants to heal that person. Sure enough, when they pray for them, they generally experience at least some measure of healing.

Dryness and Doubt

All of us experience times—some of them long and arduous—when our spiritual gas tank is on empty. Does this mean we have been captured by doubt? Perhaps. There is a dryness that comes as a result of doubting. Understanding follows obedience, and some people refuse to obey, which keeps them from understanding, which propels them into dryness.

To paraphrase MacDonald: If the words of Jesus do not seem true to you, either they are not the words of Jesus or you are not true enough yet to understand them. The mind of a person can receive any word only in the degree to which it is the word of Christ, and in the degree to which the person is one with Christ. Untruth and disunity prevent understanding.

So if your dryness exists in the presence of a lack of comprehension, the answer is to find the next word of God and put your hand to the plow by sheer obedience. Understanding and "moisture" will generally follow.

Some dryness, on the other hand, is a test. The dry one has not deserved the dryness. In fact, he or she has been obedient to the point that God has built upon that obedience with a little dryness. Dryness is never God's goal, merely His means to a better goal. What do you do then? The same as when the dryness comes because of disobedience: Just keep obeying the next word God brings to your attention. Do it out of willful rather than emotional love for Him. Persevere. Keep on keeping on. You will come out of it.

Fear and Doubt

Having fear is an example of Satan's access to our emotions. The point of the fear is to get you to back off from the things of God. In such cases, faith is spelled *c-o-u-r-a-g-e*. Courage is willful trust in God despite adverse circumstances and one's feelings about them.

I hate fear. I just hate it. But following Jesus Christ around is almost guaranteed to produce fear on a fairly regular basis. We fear that something will not work—prayers for healing, for example. We fear that nothing will happen. We fear that people will be hurt by our mistakes. We fear that we will look like fools. We fear that others will not respond well to us. And you know what? These are legitimate fears!

But let me tell you something: Fear is almost a guarantee that God wants to do something good.

I think of the priests who carried the Ark of the Covenant under Joshua's leadership, leading a million and a half Israelites into the Promised Land. All they had to do was step into the Jordan River and it would divide, allowing them and all the Israelites to walk across to Canaan on dry ground. How do you think they felt, standing on the banks of the swift-flowing Jordan? I am sure they felt afraid. They probably feared not drowning but looking dumb—and wet! Maybe they feared that the waters would not divide, that Joshua had not heard accurately from the Lord what they were to do, that they were not faithful enough. But they had the willful courage to step forward. And once they put their feet into motion, God acted.

They are no more special than you in His sight.

If we are never afraid, we are probably insulating ourselves from challenges we need to face. Never to be afraid is to have plateaued, gone stale. It is to be sitting on our lees. The Moabites were chastised by God through the prophet Jeremiah because they were "at rest from youth, like wine left on its dregs, not poured from one jar to another. . . . So she tastes as she did, and her aroma is unchanged" (Jeremiah 48:11). The Moabites fled challenges, preferred the easy way—just lying around. But they did not mature and their dregs polluted their flavor. A little fear now and then is a sign that you are growing.

In the next chapter we will look into a dynamic that is so much a part of our society that we may not even recognize it as an enemy of faith.

9
Flying Solo

The last enemy of faith I want to discuss is flying solo. In Western civilization, and in America in particular, we maintain a long-standing admiration for loners. Our culture venerates the can-do, stand-alone, rely-on-yourself qualities of the trapper, the mountain man, the Marlboro Man, James Bond, the Lone Ranger. If you need others, you are a wimp. "Whatsamatter, you can't take care of yourself?"

Even if we know better, something in us still rises to the challenge to declare our independence. Even if we know we cannot get along by ourselves, something in us may still want to.

An African clergyman once visited a prayer group I was leading. Since I wanted to hear his perspective on America, I asked him what he had noticed about us.

"Your loneliness," he replied immediately.

Of all the things I expected him to say, that was not it.

"What do you mean?" I asked, stunned.

"In my country it would be unthinkable for a person to live alone in an apartment, even if they could afford it. Why would they choose such isolation? Why would they cut themselves off from their family and friends?"

Suddenly a window opened and I saw something I had not seen before—a picture of what togetherness might mean. I was both attracted and repelled by that picture. Something in me longed for the quality of togetherness that I glimpsed, yet something else in me felt claustrophobic about never being able to be alone. I have been working with that tension ever since.

I am writing this book with the assumption that faith is a relationship. As I believe in and interact with God, I am in relationship with Him. What's more, the quality of that relationship is distinctly *dependent*. I have mentioned this before, but I emphasize again that this dynamic goes all the way back to our Founder, who said, "The Son *can do nothing by himself*; he can do only what he sees his Father doing, because whatever the Father does the Son also does" (John 5:19, italics mine). Jesus was declaring His absolute dependence on the Father for everything He needed for life and ministry. Ten chapters later He applied the same truth to us: "Apart from me *you can do nothing*" (15:5, italics mine).

What was true of Jesus as He related to the Father is true of us as we relate to Jesus. He modeled dependence for us. He thought of dependence as a virtue—the best way to get things done. In fact, *can do nothing* indicates that Jesus knew dependence was the only way to get things done. As if that were not enough, He taught that this dependence should be lateral as well as vertical. He wants us to be as tied in with one another as we are with Him. In fact, there is a real sense in which Jesus conceals Himself from us except through one another.

Being Part of a Community

A couple of years after I was renewed in my Christian life, on a day early in January, the Lord said to me, *I'm not going to heal you through your own prayers if you get sick this year.*

And He didn't. I know, because I prayed for myself for healing every time I got a cold or a raw throat or the flu and it didn't work. But He healed me quickly when I let others pray for me.

God wanted me to grow in dependence on others rather than in independence from them. He thinks (contrary to our Western values) that it is a virtue to need other people.

In fact, it is worth asking a key question about Paul's use of the term *body* to describe the Church: Is *body* a figure of speech or an actual reality? In physical terms, of course, it is a figure of speech, for it is clear that you are not a physical elbow. But when we reply that Paul's use of the term *body* is true in a spiritual sense, let's watch out when we use the word *spiritual* lest we mean *unreal*. The spiritual realm is absolutely real, and the Bible says we are members of one Body—the Lord's Body (1 Corinthians 12). Spiritually it is not only undesirable but impossible to be a Lone Ranger, for one organ cannot perform the combined functions of the other organs. No matter how good an eye sees, it cannot hear.

In the community of the Body of Christ, the good things of God are contagious. When you see real love at work, it makes you want to be more loving yourself. When a truly gentle person comes into view, you want to emulate that person's qualities. God has organized us that way.

The triune Godhead is the example of this "co-inhering" or mutual indwelling—one God in three Persons. The oneness is the essential unity that the Persons of the Godhead share in common. The threeness is what makes Them able to relate in love. Love requires plurality: There must be lover, beloved and the love between them. The Trinity is a community. The Father is Lover and Beloved of the Son and the Holy Spirit. The Son is Lover and Beloved of the Father and the Holy Spirit. The Holy Spirit is Lover and Beloved of the Father and the Son. Together, in Their oneness, the Word says, "God is love." So God (He, They) is (are) a community, the divine community. And the divine community is the model for the human community.

Not the model only, but also the resource. As Peter observes,

> Thus he has given us, through these things, his precious and very great promises, so that through them you may escape from the corruption that is in the world because of lust, and may become *participants of the divine nature.*
> 2 Peter 1:4, NRSV (italics mine)

God allows and invites us to partake in His very nature, His divine community. But you *alone* are not so invited, only you *together.* It is only as we link completely with one another that we may manifest and participate in the divine community.

When it comes to growing in faith, therefore, we cannot progress in isolation from others. Nor can I compete with you in the race for superior faith because that would be like my eye competing with my ear. They are not opposed; they need each other. You bring your temperament, experience, knowledge, wisdom, insights and gifts to our relationship, which I cannot get in any other way than by being in relationship with you, and which are extremely useful to my growth in faith. I bring mine in turn to you. Together you and I provide these things for one another as we both grow in faith:

Modeling: We demonstrate for one another how truths are lived out.

Understanding: We help one another comprehend truths we have not yet digested.

Strength: When we are feeling down, we help to buck one another up, activate our wills and go on going on.

Inspiration: We help each other to gain the courage to stretch in our own experience of faith.

Correction: We show one another gently where we may be off-course.

And that spells *music!* We make the Lord's music together, each contributing to one another the notes that only we can bring.

You know, of course, that it takes both the black and white keys on a piano to make music. Paul said that Jesus Christ has broken down all the walls between the usual things that divide us:

Black or white or brown or yellow
Male or female
Jew or Gentile
Rich or poor
Young or old
Professional or lay
New in faith or old in faith

Underline the seven words that apply to you. They represent a composite of obvious factors that you can bring to a faith-enhancing relationship with another believer. When you add the things mentioned above—temperament, experience, knowledge, wisdom, insights and gifts, you total up to an irreplaceable, priceless, unique opportunity who can help another grow as nothing and no one else can.

Let's look at some specific ways we can help one another to grow in faith.

Synergism

This is an English word straight out of the Greek: *syn*, together, and *ergos*, work. It means that things working together achieve more than they can separately.

Did you ever play cribbage? One pair of cards is worth two points; three of the same are worth six points. Add just one more card and the value doubles to twelve points. Think of how much twelve working together are worth! That is synergism.

In the Bible, twelve is the number for community—twelve tribes, twelve disciples. Sociologists tell you that you can get to know and work well with about eleven other people. You twelve working together, guided by and having the faith of God, can produce prodigiously. You cannot have that quality of relationship with your whole church; it is too big. But you can have it with any number up to a dozen or so.

The small group movement sweeping churches today around the world is both a *be* and a *do* kind of thing. Small groups help us more effectively to *be* the kind of people God is calling us to be, and they help us to *do* the works of God with vastly greater authority, power and results. When we are in a synergistic relationship, we discover an astonishingly vigorous dynamic.

Some people, for example, are what I call "doors of visitation"—people whose giftedness releases the giftedness of others. My friend Lloyd has great faith that people will be filled with the Holy Spirit when he prays for them. And you know what? My faith for that increases when I am in Lloyd's presence. For my part, I have a nearly effortless faith that joint problems will be healed. Other people seem to catch that faith in my presence.

"One man [can] chase a thousand," as Deuteronomy 32:30 puts it synergistically, "or two put ten thousand to flight." If you want to take this statement literally, two are

five times more effective working together than separately.

So I ask you: Who are you in a deepening working relationship with?

Mutuality

Mutuality differs somewhat from synergism. Rather
than a multiplying of forces, mutuality is a trading of burdens. "Carry each other's burdens," wrote Paul, "and in
this way you will fulfill the law of Christ" (Galatians 6:2).
What is the "law of Christ"? To love each other. In order
to fulfill the law of love, we should be involved in the kind
of relationships in which we can exchange burdens.

I have known the Lord to take a burden from someone
who just *had* to function and place it on a friend who
could afford to carry the burden for a time. The second
carried the weight of the concern for a while so the first
could function unencumbered.

Hard Questions About Faith

*Number Ten: When should we, like the im-
portunate widow, pray for something repeatedly, and when is that tantamount to
vain repetition or an attempt to manipulate
God? And where does faith enter in?*

Since I seem to have a gift of faith concerning joints, I
can exercise faith for someone else's need in that area.
Someone with faith concerning finances might, in turn,
carry my burden for a fiscal need. I learned years ago that
people with emotional damage often need someone else

to have faith for their inner healing. Yes, I know that faith is an act of the will, but it is a relief not to have to counter negative emotions produced by past traumas in order to exercise faith for healing. You do not carry the same baggage as I do about my past, so you can wade into those memories unencumbered by negative emotions, and can therefore exercise faith more easily than I.

Does God want you to do that for me? You bet.

What this means is that there are some areas of life in which I may never have effective faith, except as it is available to me through you. There are some things God may never give me faith for except through you. So I had better stay close to you, open to you, clear with you, or I will experience a significant lack in my life.

Will you trust those in your life enough to tell them honestly what you need their faith for? Will you invite those persons to trust you enough to share their needs with you? What is easy for you to believe? What is hard? What is easy for your friend in the church to believe? What is hard?

I want to challenge you to answer these questions because Christianity was never intended to be a solo flight. Pre-Christianity was not a solo flight either. Some things, you know, cross the line between the Old and New Testaments. Faith is one of them.

The story of the Shunammite woman is a great example of someone who knew she needed help in order to believe and get her faith answered. If you remember the story (2 Kings 4), this childless woman extended hospitality to the prophet Elisha by building a guest room for him on the roof of her home. In gratitude Elisha heard the Lord tell him to predict that she would have a child the next year.

Then one day, when that child was old enough to work in the fields with his father, he became sick, complaining of pain in his head. A few hours later he died. His mother's response is a sophisticated and instructive example of faith.

First she laid her son's body on the bed of Elisha. She wanted his body to be in contact with something that had been in contact with Elisha. She seemed to know intuitively that the release of faith often involves some physical point of contact.

Second, she made immediate plans to get to Elisha. She knew he was a man of God and that it was by Elisha's word that God had granted her a son. In her terrible crisis, it was natural that she would think of him, and she went to elicit his help.

Third, she refused to state the problem flatly to her husband. When he asked why she wanted to go to the prophet, she replied, "It's all right." It *wasn't* all right. Was she just "in denial," as we say today? Maybe. Or maybe she had communication problems with her husband. But I suspect that something more sophisticated was going on. In the face of horrible contrary evidence, the Shunammite woman was expressing her faith and "seeing" its successful outcome. She was believing everything would turn out all right. This is also what Jesus did, remember, in the Lazarus episode when He said, "Our friend Lazarus has fallen asleep; but I am going there to wake him up" (John 11:11). Was Jesus in denial? No, He was already seeing the result of His faith. When Elisha, seeing her in the distance, sent his servant Gehazi to ask her if everything was O.K., again her response was "Everything is all right."

Fourth, even when she came face-to-face with Elisha, still she did not state the problem clearly. She took hold of his feet and said, "Did I ask you for a son, my lord? Didn't I tell you, 'Don't raise my hopes'?"

Fifth, she was not accepting any alternate solutions to her decision that Elisha himself was going to help her. When Elisha dispatched Gehazi to take his staff and put it on the face of the child, her response was to use a for-mula oath, "As surely as the LORD lives and as you live, I will not leave you." Elisha alone had what she needed—contact with God—and she was not letting go of him.

From that point Scripture makes no more comment on her role in the exercise of faith. The focus of the story shifts to Elisha and what he did to bring the boy back to life. You can bet that the woman was praying downstairs like mad, of course, while Elisha was up in his room praying for the boy, but the Bible does not say so. From its point of view, her job was done once she linked her faith to that of the one who could help her. Together this woman and Elisha got the job done; they believed God for the reversal of a catastrophe. "Two [can] put ten thousand to flight. . . ."

When *you* are in a catastrophe, put the call out for prayer everywhere you can. Get hold of the most believ-ing, most anointed people you can and constrain them to take steps to help you. This is not a time for business-as-usual—not for you *or* for those who can help you—for this is the nature of the Body: "If one part suffers, *every* part suffers with it" (1 Corinthians 12:26, italics mine). The Shunammite woman did not accept Elisha's busi-ness-as-usual response, which was to send someone else. She insisted that he hear her request for his presence and action. And she prevailed.

I have to admit, I do not like being put into that kind of position, for it places an unexpected demand on my own faith. I never feel "up to it." And I am no great healer. So in my flesh I have been tempted—and have actually tried—to dodge the demand. But God has answered sev-eral of the demands of people who scraped up the strength to push a request into my face.

When someone says, "I swear on a stack of Bibles [our formula oath] that you are going to help me!" we tend to agree, don't we? Their sheer determination pushes aside our unsheer wish to avoid being put on the spot. We bow to the strength of their insistence. Maybe that is why Jesus taught on the value of persistence in prayer. (Remember the Syrophoenician woman in chapter 3.)

What inner quality does it require for a person to get that insistent? I think an intolerance of what ought not to be. The Syrophoenician woman refused to be reconciled to the presence of a demon in her daughter. The centurion refused to accept the oncoming death of his valued servant. The Shunammite woman refused to accept the death of her son, who had been a gift from God. The woman with the issue of blood refused to put up any longer with the life-dominating illness that had controlled her life for twelve years. Bartimaeus refused to be silent in his blindness when there was a chance the Son of David might hear and have mercy, so he set up a proper howl until he got Jesus' attention.

What are you intolerant of? What condition in your life or city or church or nation is simply unacceptable? What will you put up with no longer?

Then: Who can you go to and persuade to join you? Whose help do you absolutely have to have? Whose strength or anointing or position or experience is crucial to the success of defeating that which ought not to be?

You may have to answer questions like these only once in your life. Or you may be chosen to have to deal with them over and over. But take a lesson from the Shunammite woman, get the help you need in order to believe and get your prayer answered.

Part 4

Deeper Issues

Most of this book has been about normal faith. But in this final section we will discuss the gift of faith and how it differs from normal, everyday faith. Then we will examine the relationship between faith and freedom. And finally we will see if we can unwrap the relationship between our will and God's love.

10
The Gift
of Faith

The gift of faith is a booster shot from the Holy Spirit to help us accomplish something for which our normal faith is insufficient. It is a rising up of faith from a source beyond ourselves. It is like being laid hold of, as well as laying hold of something beyond our reach. To those experiencing it, it is one of the clearest examples of being used by God in a way that is almost automatic. It barely needs our permission and it exceeds what we ourselves would have the courage to permit.

"To each one," Paul wrote, "the manifestation of the Spirit is given for the common good. To one there is given . . . faith by the same Spirit" (1 Corinthians 12:7–9). The gift of faith may take little time or much time. In a healing it may occur quickly. In the financing of a work God wants to do, it may take quite a while. It may occur once and be gone, or it may recur several times over the duration of a need.

But before we explore the gift of faith, which is one of the spiritual gifts, let's review spiritual gifts in general.

Spiritual gifts are one of the ways God chooses to reveal Himself in human beings. Rather than just do it Himself, He does it through us. He likes to collaborate with us. He is the One who has the power, but He chooses to use His power in and for and through people. It is as though we were the copper wire for His electricity.

For most people, a spiritual gift is a supernatural enhancement of a natural ability. I could demonstrate this point easily with one of the more dramatic spiritual gifts, such as miracles. But let me try it with something not so dramatic.

My wife Sue has the gift of helps. In the natural she has highly developed common sense. She is a good observer and cares for others. But on top of this natural base, the Spirit gives her an anointing of helps. This anointing is an enrichment of her natural abilities. Her advice, for example, is sound and can help others in a greater way than can be accounted for by her natural abilities.

This anointing of helps is both a potentiality and an actualization of that potentiality, which occurs when:

1. There is a need for it.
2. The Spirit leads Sue to cooperate with Him.
3. She risks that cooperation in faith.
4. The Spirit accomplishes something through her that she could not have done alone.

Is the difference between the natural and supernatural obvious? Generally not. It takes eyes of faith to notice the hand of God at work. (Some in Jesus' time did not believe even though they saw great demonstrations of the Spirit's power through His ministry.) Nor is there much *perceptible* difference between the natural and supernatural in a person through whom a spiritual gift is being exercised.

I almost never *feel* powerful when the Spirit's power is moving through me. In fact, most of the time I feel distinctly *un*powerful or *un*spiritual. Generally I do not know that a person is being healed until he says he is or until he shows evidence that healing is taking place. In the early days my hands often got hot when people were being healed, but that phenomenon ceased. It was as though the Spirit encouraged me by that sensation until I had enough experience to believe that He wanted to heal people through me. Then the sensation pretty much ended.

How one experiences a gift depends on what the gift is and how it is being utilized. When I am operating in the word of knowledge, it tends to be rather coldly mental. I rarely feel anything. The reason for this, I have decided, is that feelings would cloud my thinking. If I started to feel some emotion about the words I was getting, my capacity to receive such words might be hampered. As it is, when I reflect later on what happened after I got and acted on a word of knowledge, I may get very emotional indeed, praising God profusely for what He did. But while I need to operate in the gift, I feel nothing.

Well, that's not quite so. I do feel something—fear! I feel afraid that the Holy Spirit is not going to come through, that I am not worthy of being used by Him, that there is some unknown reason why the gift this time is going to fail, that I have used up all the grace I could reasonably hope for. This is spiritual warfare. Remember I said that the devil has access to our emotions? Well, that is how he operates when the Spirit wants to exercise spiritual gifts through us. And you know what? God lets him get away with it, because the exercising of a spiritual gift is itself an opportunity to exercise what I am calling normal faith.

Some gifts can be exercised in a very short time—words of knowledge, prophecy, tongues, miracles, some healings. And some require a lot of time—leadership, pastoring, teaching, administration and serving.

Now let's talk about some of the ways the gift of faith works.

How It Works

A Knowing

Some people experience the gift of faith as a knowing, a certainty that comes as a gift, beyond normal faith, unbidden and uncontrollable, for the duration and purpose that suit it. When it is sudden, it can leave the person who experienced it shaken or exhilarated. This knowing is beyond reason, beyond facts, beyond explanation. It just happens and the one in whom it happens knows it. One person described it like this: "I just know it in my knower!"

Anger

Another way we may experience the gift of faith is, strangely enough, as anger.

On several occasions I have been suddenly and completely swept by anger as faith went coursing through me. The first time I ran into a demon infesting someone, I was 'way out of my league. At the point of giving up being able to do anything for this woman, I suddenly became enraged and in violent language and gesture ordered it out of her with complete authority. It obeyed instantly.

On another occasion someone was messing with the beliefs of my flock at a house gathering. I had good-naturedly observed what was going on for more than an hour. Suddenly, and without any forewarning, I uttered a barely controlled command for that person to shut up, which he immediately did. The episode was over, except for the adrenaline that the anger had set loose in my veins.

Now I must tell you that my outburst was unpremeditated. It was also embarrassing to me. I don't generally act that way. I don't *want* to act that way. It is a mystery to me why God would "sponsor" that outburst. All I know is that it was not me, that it was effective and that it did not upset anyone present. They seemed to recognize the presence of God in it.

On several occasions that anger—the anger that is a vehicle for the gift of faith—has erupted in me against illness. When that happens I feel a quick rising up in my chest of anger-force. Nearly instantly that sensation spills into my arms and comes forth from my hands, as it were, as I utter authoritative words. In every instance the person has been healed immediately.

Encouragement

When we are beset with a challenge that takes much time to meet, the gift of faith often comes at various points as en-courage-ment—a thrusting of one into courage. This blessing may come when we are at rock bottom or when we are sensing no great need. Sometimes it comes when we are alone with the Lord, at other times through the ministration of someone else.

Early in my present pastorate I was trying to make some changes in the congregation that I believed the Lord wanted. I was encountering some resistance to my efforts and was in need of encouragement. Then, during a prayer meeting, a woman rose out of her chair, put her hands on my shoulders and said a whole paragraph of words. I remember only this phrase: "Do not be afraid of their faces." In the months following, those words came to me again and again, refreshing and strengthening me to persevere on the course I had set.

Did the changes that were needed occur? Yes, thanks be to God. Was this the gift of faith? I think it was.

Doors of Visitation

Some people are, as I mentioned in the last chapter, what I call "doors of visitation"—people whose giftedness releases our own. There are people, for example, in whose inspiring, encouraging presence it is easy for me to bring God's healing to the sick. My own faith recognizes and swells under their influence, and I seem to be able to believe the Spirit for greater-than-usual results in their presence. Who has the gift of faith here, me or the "door of visitation"? It is at least me, even if the other's faith is "normal" for him or her.

When the task has been accomplished for which the gift of faith was sent, I may be back to square one for the very next need. A surge of two thousand volts quickly calms down to my normal six volts again.

Group Faith

There are glorious times when the gift of faith comes on a whole group, as we touched on in the last chapter. At such times God's Spirit moves on individuals and on the whole to release anointing, healing, repentance or unity. The participants become aware that they have been dealt with as individuals but also as a corporate body. Something synergistic occurs, creating a result greater than the sum of its parts.

You do not want to miss this for the world!

A Puzzle

There seems to be nothing I can do to make a gift of faith materialize except to put myself in situations in which I need help. I have found that the gift of faith does not manifest until *after* I have committed myself to trying to help someone. But many times when I have been almost desperate for such faith, it has not come. Why? I don't know. It is one of the areas of continuing mystery between me and God. But as we continue to deepen our relationship with God, growing in holiness and in the fruit of the Spirit, putting ourselves into situations in which we need the power of God—these things and more make us available for the gift of faith and, indeed, for any spiritual gift.

But honesty compels me to state almost the opposite as well. There have been times the gift of faith came on me

---

Hard Questions About Faith

Number Eleven: How can I know my faith is placed properly—that is to say, in God and not in some wrong object? And if God is the proper object of faith and the mover on our behalf, why did Jesus repeatedly say, "Your faith [not your God] has made you whole"?

---

when I was totally undeserving, walking in selfhood and having barely emerged from serious sin. I have had the gift of faith rise up in me when I had no hope for even a normal level of faith. There have been times it flashed up when I was dead tired and hoped for only a short encounter with someone. The mercy of God is past reckoning.

Often it has not been my gift of faith that got the job done but the person's who came to me for ministry. In fact, I have seen some remarkable healings take place in the *absence* of my faith.

What I mean to say here is that this faith stuff is a mystery and that it is supposed to be a mystery. Who would want to believe in and follow a God he or she understood perfectly? The riches of Christ are past finding out, Paul declared. If we could exhaust His truth, if we could fully compass His ways, if we could invariably predict His response, we would be as great as He.

Ownership

Who owns the gift of faith? Do spiritual gifts become our own? I don't think so. In fact, I think it is a mistake to think so.

A person can become known for a certain gift that manifests itself through him or her fairly regularly. This is because gifts are enhancements of the natural, and the natural in us does not change much. Also, many gifts take a lifetime to develop, so it would be counterproductive for the Spirit to change your gifts every six months. But the recurrence of a gift or package of gifts does not mean that you possess them. Because our God is an incarnationalist, He works through people, while His gifts remain His. Our frailty, our pride and our limited view would make it hazardous for us to own them.

So what is it that happens when spiritual gifts visit? Well, they sit on us from time to time to achieve a particular purpose in the mind of God. For that moment I carry the anointing for the target that the anointing seeks. There is a real sense in which I no longer "have" the gift once it achieves its ends.

It is not my decision to release a spiritual gift. It *is* my decision to place myself in the circumstances in which a gift is needed. But the gift remains the property and domain of the Holy Spirit. What's more, the goal of a gift is the blessing of someone else, not me. If I pray for you and you get healed, *you* get the gift of healing, not me. If teaching comes forth from me that blesses you, you rather than I were the Spirit's target.

So do I get nothing out of a gift that operates through me? Of course not. I get richly blessed to have been used by God. That fulfills me, satisfies me, pleases me. I experience growth in my understanding, encouragement, faith and relationships with God and other people each time the Spirit administrates gifts through me. So I look forward eagerly to the next occurrence of a gift operating through me.

But it is not as though the gift sits in my back pocket waiting for me to take it out and give it to someone. I own nothing but the capacity for being filled and used by the Spirit. The only thing that is really mine is my emptiness.

Using the Gift of Faith

Faith does not exist for itself. One does not receive a gift of faith just to be having faith. Faith is always faith *for* something. That something may be an illness, a problem, an impossible situation, a confusion, an alienated relationship, a financial need, an agonizing despair, a resolute opposition. It may affect your body, your mind, your emotions, your relationships, your situation. It may be short-term or long-term. It may influence relatively small matters or huge ones. It may be located in the next room or consume a whole nation across the sea.

The thing to do is exercise normal faith and expect the gift of faith to leap up when it suits God.

- Pray in accordance with your present understanding of who God is and how He works. But do not be surprised during the operation of your normal, will-based faith if the gift of faith rises up suddenly within you. Two minutes of the eruption of the gift of faith can yield more than two weeks of plodding, normal faith. But you cannot "pass Go and proceed directly" to the gift of faith. It is launched from the platform of normal faith.

- Go ahead and take action in the circumstance facing you. Do not bail out, drop out or flip out. Take your will in hand and step into the situation, telling God He must be there to help, protect, enable and guide you.

I taped a prayer onto a picture of Jesus in my office: "Lord, because You must, You shall, and I will rest in that." Whatever it is that must be done, He is the one to do it. And because He has both the capability and the desire, I can decide that He will do it. Through me, even!

A while back I mentioned the crossing of the Israelites into Canaan, and that not until the priests bearing the Ark of the Covenant stepped into the Jordan River did its waters recede, permitting the people of Israel to cross into the Promised Land. Think how much faith the priests had before the waters divided. Probably not much. But they stepped in anyway. *Then* the waters divided, and you can bet they experienced a huge surge of faith. "Attababy, *God!*" they shouted, tramping into the middle of the ex-river, taking up their posts and smiling beneficently and gleefully at the hordes passing by.

Normal faith, then the gift of faith, is how it works.

Control

We can talk about this real quick. God has control of the gift of faith; we don't. We can ask for it, but nine out of ten times He seems to think we do not need a booster shot—just regular, obedient, persevering faith.

He is *always* right. Believe that.

The Honeymoon

Many new Christians experience a period of effortless grace immediately following their conversion and/or infilling with the Holy Spirit. This version of the gift of faith may extend for several months. In my case it lasted half a year. Effortlessness is characteristic of the honeymoon with Jesus. One may experience effortless joy, effortless faith, effortless answers to prayer, effortless peace, effortless closeness to God, effortless resisting of temptation.

In His great kindness and mercy, God gives this effortlessness to His children—for a time. Inevitably the honeymoon ends. It makes no difference how it ends—through falling into sin, through trial, through mishap, through mere attrition. The point is, it ends. Why? We have visited this verse before: "Without faith it is impossible to please God" (Hebrews 11:6). When the honeymoon ends, God is saying, "Child, it is time for you to start to mature now, to begin walking—not in effortlessness but in faith. So I have withdrawn the effortlessness that I gave you. It was a love gift for a time, and that time is over."

This withdrawal of effortlessness can be a period of great confusion to the person whose honeymoon with God has ended. He may find himself doing some of the same things over and over that occurred in his conversion, trying to restart the honeymoon. He may doubt that his conversion or renewal really occurred. He may come under condemnation, either from himself or from well-meaning but misinformed Christians. He may even find confusion or condemnation in the Bible itself: "You have forsaken your first love" (Revelation 2:4). And he will probably grieve the loss of the things that before came so beautifully and easily.

This experience is probably one of the reasons Paul ordered that new believers not be placed in positions of authority: "He must not be a recent convert" (1 Timothy 3:6). They have not had time yet to work out the confusion and struggle of adapting to the loss of the honeymoon. They have not yet demonstrated that they can go on and walk the talk, so they are not yet of much use in the ministry of encouraging others.

This is a time to persevere, to refuse to give up, to defy feelings of despair, to refute thoughts of accusation. It is a time to go on going on, despite real questions and considerable confusion. This form of the gift of faith, in other words, ends in a season of toughing it out.

But freedom awaits those who continue in faith, as we will see in the next chapter.

11
Faith and Freedom

When I was still a relatively young pastor, I had a tiff with my bishop. I cannot even remember what it was about. But during the disagreement I let my head lay leader send a letter out to the congregation relating to money in which he included a sentence hostile to the bishop. When he showed me the draft of the letter, rebellion rose up in my heart and I said, "Yeah, send it!"

I forgot the bishop was on our mailing list.

Two days later my phone rang. It was my immediate superior—who is called in our denomination an archdeacon—whose office in downtown L.A. was just across the hall from the bishop's. Instantly I could see what had happened. The bishop had read his mail, marched across the hall to the archdeacon and said, "Look what one of your vicars just put out."

My superior began eagerly to chew up my side, excoriating me not only for the recent gaff but for former complaints as well. As I listened I swept the pile of papers on my desk off onto the floor, grabbed a clean sheet of paper and began scribbling furious notes for my defense.

Suddenly a thought came into my mind, so loud that I was shocked: I *justified you.*

As I tried to comprehend this, I said almost absently, "What?" which made the archdeacon repeat his last point.

But I wasn't listening to him now. My mind was reeling with New Testament phrases: *Justified through faith, God who justifies the wicked, The righteousness that is by faith.* As the doctrine of justification by faith swirled through my mind, I found myself thinking, *You mean that stuff is real?* It was not that I doubted it; I just had not yet really experienced it.

As I was struggling to grasp all this, the thought-voice came again: *Well, didn't I justify you?*

I wanted more time to ponder this. But my boss' voice was continuing to chew on me and I knew I needed to make a response to him and to the voice of the Lord. So I said, this time in my mind, *Well, uh, yes, Lord, I guess You did justify me.*

Immediately: *Then you don't have to justify yourself, do you?*

Uh, I guess not.

End of transmission.

Just then I heard my superior say, "Well, what do you have to say for yourself, young man?"

"Sir, everything you have said is absolutely correct. I humbly apologize for the embarrassment I've caused you and the bishop. I ask your forgiveness. And I pledge that nothing like this will occur in the future." And I meant it.

He forgave me and rang off.

I walked into the church sanctuary expecting to be plunged at any minute into depression, for that had been my pattern whenever I had been found out. I waited, but no depression came. Instead a mysterious joy welled up from deep within me and spilled out in praises and laughs and exuberant expressions of glee. For thirty minutes I skipped up and down the aisles like a newborn lamb that has discovered its legs in a mountain meadow. It was as though I had been born again *again*. Perhaps I had!

And that is exactly what justification by faith means. It means we do not have to justify ourselves. It means we can honestly admit our mistakes. It means we can appropriate the payment for our errors and sins that Jesus made on the cross. It means we do not have to pretend we are better than we are. It means we do not have to walk in denial. It means we do not have to come to self-acceptance on a performance basis. It means we are *free*—free from condemnation; from the accusation of our consciences; from the judgments of others; from the predictive nature of our past sins by which they threaten to repeat themselves. Free, free, free!

The good news is better news than we had thought. Salvation, justification, redemption—whatever word you want to use, it is a *gift!* You cannot earn or pay back God's gifts. All you can do is receive them and walk in them— gratefully, humbly, exuberantly, for you have been freed to be grateful and humble and joyful.

Seven Elements of Freedom

Freedom is an interior standing with God that affects everything about us. Freedom is both a means and a goal: "It is for freedom that Christ has set us free. Stand firm, then, and do not let yourselves be burdened again by a yoke of slavery" (Galatians 5:1).

Let's look at seven components in the relationship between faith and freedom. Getting these seven factors straight is an immense help in the business of having effective faith.

1. Law

Law is the definer of sin. Law is the Ten Commandments. Law is the teachings of Jesus, especially in the Sermon on the Mount (Matthew 5–7). "Apart from law, sin is dead" (Romans 7:8). If you want to know if you are a sinner, read the Law; it will tell you. God's purpose in giving us the Law, however, is not to freeze us in its judgment but to release us from its condemnation.

The Law reveals to us the condition of our hearts, showing us where we are sinful, guilty and incapable of self-reformation. The Law brings us to the awareness that we need a Savior. Finally, the Law is our guide for grateful response once we have been saved.

2. Grace

When we confront the Law, allowing it to point out the sin in our lives, we are moved to cry, "Help!" It is at that point that the Spirit of God comes, bringing cleansing to our hearts. Because Christ was sinless, He qualified to be the sacrifice for sin. He hung on the cross for six hours. You and I could hang there for six years and it would not pay off a single sin because we do not qualify as a sacrifice for sin. You have to be sinless for that.

Someone made an acronym out of the word *grace: Gifts Received At Christ's Expense.* The first and greatest gift is justification, which puts you in good standing with God for all eternity.

3. Justification

Justification is a two-way transaction. You might describe it as an exchange—a central dynamic of the saving work of Christ. We see this clearly in 2 Corinthians 5:21: "God made him who had no sin to be sin for us, so that in him we might become the righteousness of God."

The dimensions of this exchange are staggering. The sinless Jesus became the fact of sin itself so that sinful people could be divested of their sins and invested with the righteousness of God.

Jesus gives us His standing; we give Him ours. That exchange is not fair but it is just. The justice of God has to be satisfied. He cannot simply wink at sin and injustice; they must be paid for. His love arranged the sacrifice of His Son, the only one who could pay the price. His love goes even further than merely satisfying the requirements of the negative. It goes so far as to accord us the benefits of the positive—His Son's righteousness.

4. Healing

A further benefit of exchange is the healing of the conditions brought on us by sin. "He himself bore our sins in his body on the tree, so that we might die to sins and live for righteousness; by his wounds you have been healed" (1 Peter 2:24). Here Peter agrees with Paul's assessment of the dimensions of the exchange, adding the concept of healing to that of justification: The unwounded Jesus got wounded and our wounds get healed. This is precisely what the messianic predictions of Isaiah 53 asserted: "He was pierced for our transgressions, he was crushed for our iniquities; the punishment that brought us peace was upon him, and by his wounds we are healed" (verse 5).

The healing of our bodies, souls, spirits and relationships becomes discoverable and accessible through the release of our faith.

5. Flesh and Spirit

The word *flesh* in the New Testament does not always have a negative connotation, but it does in the context of the struggle between flesh and spirit. Flesh is the man or woman whose fallen nature gets him or her into trouble.

Flesh is his natural mind, her unsanctified emotions, his fallen will, her unregenerate spirit (or her spirit that has been regenerated but is ignored). Paul gives a long, graphic list of behaviors and characteristics produced by the flesh: "Sexual immorality, impurity and debauchery; idolatry and witchcraft; hatred, discord, jealousy, fits of rage, selfish ambition, dissensions, factions and envy; drunkenness, orgies, and the like" (Galatians 5:19–21). Bad stuff.

Then he lists wonderful things that the Spirit produces in us: "Love, joy, peace, patience, kindness, goodness, faithfulness, gentleness and self-control" (verses 22–23). Don't miss the last line of verse 23: "Against such things there is no law."

The Law is allowed to scrutinize the acts of the flesh but not of the Spirit. If you are acting out of your flesh, the Law has the right to examine your behavior and condemn you for your sins. But if you are acting out of your relationship with the Holy Spirit, the Law has nothing at all to do with you. It has no right to examine you, much less judge you. You might think of the Law as a roof over your head until you receive and walk in the Spirit, at which point you have stepped outside into the sunshine. Now the roof is over there, where you used to be, but not here where you are now. You are not under the Law anymore.

The moment you regress and begin walking in the flesh, of course, the Law is right there to perform its functions: scrutiny, judgment, motivating you to seek forgiveness. And once you have confessed and been forgiven, the Law resumes its final role: guiding you to respond thankfully to the One who saved you.

6. Faith

Faith seizes the truth of justification, releasing us from the accusations of the world, the flesh and the devil. Faith applies what God has said is true of us. Faith refutes the accusations that contradict the truths God makes available to us. Faith is a new set of lenses through which we can look at ourselves and the world and everything else. And, finally, faith determines whether we are walking in the flesh or the Spirit.

7. Freedom

Freedom is the result of all the foregoing factors. You can use your freedom in two ways. First, to choose to act out of the flesh and produce a sin. Second, to act out of the Spirit and walk in the righteousness that Christ exchanged for you on the cross. This freedom is more than freedom *from*; it is also freedom *for*. In Christ we are free from the allegations and memories of the past, free for the new life He continually holds out for us.

Let's relate these factors to the experience I mentioned at the beginning of this chapter—okaying the letter hostile to the bishop.

- *Law.* The Law criticized my act of rebellion in permitting that letter to be mailed.
- *Grace.* The Lord offered me a resolution that had cost him His death and that would cost me mere honesty.
- *Justification.* The Lord counted me as "Not guilty!" He declared that He had made the whole thing right.
- *Healing.* Instead of experiencing depression, I experienced release from depression, which is a healing of the soul.
- *Flesh and spirit.* My flesh was reburied in the tomb of Christ, while I was raised to a reestablished cooperation and walk with the Spirit.
- *Faith.* Faith was the dynamic by which I could decide to be honest with my boss, respond in

courage to the input from the Lord, receive His justification of me and walk again in the Spirit.

* *Freedom.* All the above adds up to freedom. I was free—enabled—to experience the deep, delicious joy of the Spirit; to further the level of self-acceptance that comes each time we let God accept us over some real issue; to refrain from falling into that sin again; to profit from this new memory of the grace of God operating in my life.

Perfect Freedom

There is a line in *The Book of Common Prayer* about God that goes, ". . . Whom to serve is perfect freedom." Here is one of those wonderful incongruities in life. Freedom (we think in our shallowness) should allow us to do whatever we want. But true freedom is always the result of a relationship of dependence and servitude. A century-old hymn of the Church says, "Make me a captive, Lord, and then I shall be free." St. Augustine's way of putting it was this: "Love God and do what you want."

If we do love God, we will be doing what He wants us

Hard Questions About Faith

Number Twelve: Doesn't God reward faith and punish lack of faith, thus reinforcing legalism—the benefit of works?

to do. But, marvel above marvels, we will find ourselves *wanting* to do what He wants!

Faith is the crowbar that gets us from where we are to that freedom that God desires for us. Faith pries us loose from our fear and selfishness. It takes us in hand and bends our will to obey God's will. It opens our hands to the good things of God. It helps us to trust. It launches us into a freedom that no one can take from us. It is the prime example of how we lose our lives and free God to give us our lives. Faith is delicious vulnerability to the King of Heaven, who rejoices to respond to our faith by giving us a freedom that plumbs the very bottom of our souls. It allows Jesus to give us His own freedom. Was there ever a freer man who walked this earth?

This is why Paul pummeled the Galatians for having surrendered some of the freedom Christ had won for them. As I quoted earlier in this chapter, "It is for freedom that Christ has set us free. Stand firm, then, and do not let yourselves be burdened again by a yoke of slavery" (Galatians 5:1). The Galatians had allowed some unfree preachers to tie them up in the very kind of legalism Jesus died and rose again to destroy. This disturbed Paul because slavery was masquerading as faith. Legalism is fake faith. The trick is to avoid legalism while finding true servitude.

Freedom and Authority

I am almost reluctant to include the final section of this chapter because it can be difficult to grasp. I am not sure I understand it much myself. But I seem to be led to leave it in, so I repeat the advice I offered at the beginning of part 3: Eat any meat in it and spit out the bones.

There are at least two things to be said about freedom and authority. In terms of experience, first of all, God can give you freedom to the degree that you have authority.

When Sue and I were raising our sons, we could give them freedom to the degree that they had grown into authority. With authority, freedom would keep them free. Without authority, freedom would result in slavery. So we tried to model and teach them about responsibility. Every time they demonstrated responsibility, we responded by giving them more freedom in their decision-making. They could determine their own study times, for instance, if they had shown themselves responsible about getting their studies done on previous occasions. Authority qualified them for freedom.

The second thing to say about freedom and authority sounds almost like an inversion of the first point: God can give you authority to the degree that you are free. The more we appropriate who Jesus Christ is and what He has done for us, the greater the freedom in which we walk. The freer we are, the more authority God can entrust to us. That is, freedom is what qualifies us for authority, because freedom shows that a heart has been touched by the love and grace of God, and because its freedom is the proper pedestal on which to deposit authority.

Freedom leading to authority is vastly more important than authority leading to freedom. The Gospel is a message of freedom. Over and over, preachers like those who messed with the Galatians represent the Gospel as legalism, as a confinement rather than an expansion, as a death-dealer rather than a life-giver. In reality the Gospel is a message of freedom—freedom from the Law, freedom from the flesh, freedom from the world, freedom from religion, freedom from everyone and everything that is less than God Himself. "It is for freedom that Christ has set us free" because freedom is the quality that reveals Him most and characterizes the person to whom He can delegate the most authority. The truly free are the truly powerful. They can be entrusted with power and it will not twist them.

Even more, it is only the increasingly free who realize that authority is being made available to them. Freedom itself is the ears by which to hear the word of authority God speaks to us. And understanding one's authority is what permits the power of God to flow through us. This is why Paul defended his ministry—his authority—by appealing to the demonstrations of the Spirit's power that were the proof of that authority:

> My message and my preaching were not with wise and persuasive words, but with *a demonstration of the Spirit's power*, so that your faith might not rest on men's wisdom, but on God's power.
>
> 1 Corinthians 2:4–5 (italics mine)

> I will not venture to speak of anything except what Christ has accomplished through me in leading the Gentiles to obey God by what I have said and done—by *the power of signs and miracles,* through the power of the Spirit.
>
> Romans 15:18–19 (italics mine)

> I became a servant of this gospel by the gift of God's grace given me through the *working of his power.*
>
> Ephesians 3:7 (italics mine)

> ... our gospel came to you not simply with words, but also with *power.*
>
> 1 Thessalonians 1:5 (italics mine)

When challenging others, Paul declared,

> I will come to you very soon, if the Lord is willing, and then I will find out not only how these arrogant people are talking, but what *power* they have. For the kingdom of God is not a matter of talk but of *power.*
>
> 1 Corinthians 4:19–20 (italics mine)

Power demonstrates freedom. It is the proof that one has appropriated freedom. Increasing freedom must be what beckons us further and further into the heart of God.

The ticket to increasing freedom is having faith. The person growing in faith is entering the freedom in which the Spirit can apportion power and authority.

12

Sovereign Will, Inexorable Love

The problem: We have been talking throughout this book about the fact that faith is willful. We have assumed that a human being's will, though it may pull a little to one side or the other, is in general alignment with God's will. But what about a will opposed to God's? Or one not motivated to pursue God's will? Or one that cares little what God's will is? Or does not have the strength or ability to bend itself to conform to God's?

Generally when we use the word *sovereign*, we apply it to God or the Constitution or something obviously greater than we are. But I want to postulate here that the will of *each person* is sovereign, because God has designed it so.

If your will were not sovereign, God would not need to present you with teaching or exhortation or encouragement or example or promise or warning or anything else that could be described as an appeal. If your will were not sovereign, God would not have to appeal to you at all; He would just command you and that would be that.

Why the Will Is Sovereign

Let me borrow a story from a few decades ago, from George Tittmann's book *What Manner of Love*:

Once upon a time, there was a puppeteer. His skill was great and the sensitivity of his heart was past the telling. He was able to fashion innumerable little puppets, portraying in endless variety all the various types of men earth knows. He could probe deeply into the lives of his little creatures and weave the most subtle and complex of plots. And so he passed his days, his marvelous imagination playing with the puppets, fashioning story after story of infinite intricacy and fascination.

Now, as time passed, a sadness came slowly to overshadow this man and his works. The puppeteer began to realize how everything he was doing was an empty enterprise in fakery. Nothing really happened. It was as if he were playing in a mirror. With all the make-believe, nothing happened that was not really only the reflection of his own mind. He was alone in a world that, except for himself, was utterly still. No events took place. Nothing he vividly, expertly, pretended took place made anything in the least different from what it had been before. Because in so many ways he was a great puppeteer, the very excellence of his dramatic art accentuated his loneliness. The more masterful and subtle the execution of his talents, the more he felt himself silhouetted against the background of nothingness.

It happened one night that he had a vision. An angelic being offered him a chalice containing the elixir of life, one drop of which would give life to anything it touched. The possibilities of the situation were instantly apparent to him. His heart beat quickly as his trembling hand reached forth to take the offered cup. And at that moment a sudden fear came over him. His hand dropped to his side. This new thought that stole, unbidden, over his joy—do we sense what it was? Is life to be given this casually? Shall there be no anxious thought about the outcome of this giving? If he is to give life to his puppets, what guarantee will he have that they will be his friends, turn to him in welcome, submission, gratitude, and love? Can he be sure, if they become independent, that they will pay any attention to him at all? Might it not be that if they are set free to be his friends, they will turn against him instead? Is he willing to exchange being alone for being hated—or, perhaps worse, for being surrounded by indifference? The dark thought spread its shadow. Somber became the prospect and anguished his soul. As he withdrew his hand, shaking his head, he murmured to himself (for that was once again all he had to speak to), "I cannot take the chance."

The human will is sovereign because God is love. He *did* take the chance. If He were not love, He might not care whether we loved Him or not. Because He is love, He cares passionately whether we respond to Him in love. But that means, as the puppeteer discovered, that we must be free *not* to love Him.

What kind of love would forced love be? Would you want to be married to someone who did not want to be married to you, but over whom you had power to coerce into the marriage? Of course not. You want to be desired for yourself, not because you could force your spouse's allegiance.

Love must set the beloved free to love or not love in return, else the love given or returned is not real love. If God's love came to us and forced a response, it would not be love. It might be compassion or superior wisdom (though I doubt it), but it could not be love. Love sets people free; then it sets out to woo the beloved into a loving response. And the love we give back to God cannot be real love unless it is given freely. Unfree love may be respect or fear or submission, but it cannot be love.

If I cannot choose *not* to love God, I cannot choose to love Him. Love is necessarily a decision. That means that God Himself—and all "lessors"—are placed in the role of supplicants. The most any of us can do is appeal to the will of one another. The will is sovereign.

One Easter Sunday morning when I was in seminary, my family slid into the pew of a stately Southern church a few minutes before the worship service began. My three-year-old son, Kevin, suddenly stood up on the pew, looked around and asked with a loud voice, "Where's Jesus?"

"Hush!" replied his mortified parents.

"I want to see Jesus!"

"Sit down and be quiet!"

"Where's Jesus?" he demanded again.

So we forced him to sit down by pressing our hands on his head, and we imposed silence by stern and imperious looks.

After a moment he said, "I'm still standing up inside!"

Exactly so. Who do you think won that little skirmish? Kevin did. His will was in disagreement with the behavior we were imposing on him, and we all knew it.

Inexorable Love

Why am I applying the adjective *inexorable* to God's love? My thesaurus gives these synonyms for inexorable: "Inevitable, definite, determined, fixed, foregone, irrevocable, ordained, predestined, unalterable, unavoidable, unchangeable." Those are good secular approximations of biblical concepts:

The earth is full of his unfailing love.
                    Psalm 33:5

Many waters cannot quench love; rivers cannot wash it
away.

Song of Solomon 8:7

I have loved you with an everlasting love.

Jeremiah 31:3

As the Father has loved me, so have I loved you.

John 15:9

But God demonstrates his own love for us in this: While
we were still sinners, Christ died for us.

Romans 5:8

I am convinced that neither death nor life, neither angels
nor demons, neither the present nor the future, nor any
powers, neither height nor depth, nor anything else in all
creation, will be able to separate us from the love of God
that is in Christ Jesus our Lord.

Romans 8:38–39

This is how we know what love is: Jesus Christ laid down
his life for us.

1 John 3:16

Unfailing, unquenchable, everlasting, heavenly, unde-
served, undefeatable, immeasurably costly—this is how
Scripture describes God's love for us. In essence God's love
says, "I must not be defeated." Does it say that out of arro-
gance or pride? No, out of caring. "It would break my
heart," Love says, "for me to go thwarted." Love seeks the
welfare of the beloved at unspeakable cost to itself. Love
cares so yearningly for the beloved that it will not tolerate
conclusive blockages of its blessings upon the beloved. It
is not for itself but for the beloved that Love is inexorable.

The description in 1 Corinthians 13 of love resonates
with and is meant to demonstrate God's love:

Love is patient, love is kind. It does not envy, it does not boast, it is not proud. It is not rude, it is not self-seeking, it is not easily angered, it keeps no record of wrongs. Love does not delight in evil but rejoices with the truth. It always protects, always trusts, always hopes, always perseveres.

verses 4–7

That is how God loves us. According to these descriptions His love sounds gentle and genteel, which it is. But the love of God is also inexorable, the toughest thing in all the universe. What does that mean? It means we are not going to get away with refusing it.

Inexorable love is irrevocably determined to outwait, outsmart, outmaneuver, outlast, outrun and outlove the beloved's resistance to it. You talk about the "hound of heaven"—you ain't seen nothin' yet! Love says to us, "You *will* agree with Me. You *will* receive Me. You *will* let Me change you. You *will* grow up."

Let's say that every time we are presented with a choice, Love holds out the possibility of a response that could score a ten. Let's say that we respond at the level of a three. Love accepts that response and in its genius and persistence holds out another ten-level choice. We respond this time at, say, a minus five. Love accepts that response and in its genius and persistence holds out another ten-level choice. We manage to respond this time with a plus seven. Love accepts that response and in its genius and persistence holds out another ten-level choice. Finally we achieve a ten. Love accepts that response and in its genius and persistence holds out another ten-level choice.

You are getting tired of that sentence, aren't you? But God never tires of giving us another opportunity to respond in fullness to Him—and to the fullness of Him. His resourcefulness is so great that it outlasts our resistance to it. Read again those descriptions in 1 Corinthians 13 and put *God* in place of *love*. God is patience itself.

He is persistence *par excellence.* He has done the literal utmost to keep no record of our wrongs. He will never abandon hope for our welfare.

Thus, while God regards man's will as sovereign, He seems to enjoy the challenge of working in the details of our lives so that we are brought regularly to the point of decision for Him again and again and again.

Coping with Inexorable Love

We must talk about discipline. Who among us relishes being disciplined? But discipline comes to us from a loving Father whether we like it or not.

> Endure hardship as discipline; God is treating you as sons. For what son is not disciplined by his father? If you are not disciplined (and everyone undergoes discipline), then you are illegitimate children and not true sons.
>
> Hebrews 12:7–8

So discipline is going to happen! We must realize that discipline—the mark of childhood—is motivational rather than punitive. As I have said before, God already punished One for everything you will ever do that is wrong. He is not interested in punishing you. But He is intensely interested in motivating you to take your will and bend it in agreement with His. He is determined that you grow up into the daughterhood or sonship in which He has chosen to relate with you.

We need to make another clear distinction between forgiveness and restitution (a form of discipline). Forgiveness is a free gift based on Christ's sacrifice and victory, and it is given to us as we give it to others. Restitution is a payment based on justice, and it is demanded of us by the righteousness of God. Forgiveness deals with guilt while restitution deals with consequences.

Listen to what Jesus said:

> Settle matters quickly with your adversary who is taking you to court. Do it while you are still with him on the way, or he may hand you over to the judge, and the judge may hand you over to the officer, and you may be thrown into prison. I tell you the truth, you will not get out until you have paid the last penny.
>
> Matthew 5:25–26

Jesus is telling us to make matters right with others for our own benefit. Listen to George MacDonald in his sermon "The Last Farthing":

> Arrange what claim lies against you; compulsion waits behind it. Do at once what you must do one day. As there is no escape from payment, escape at least the prison that will enforce it. Do not drive justice to extremities. Duty is imperative; it must be done. It is useless to think to escape the eternal law of things: yield of yourself, nor compel God to compel you.

Would God compel you? I do not know where or what the prison is that Jesus mentions, but whatever it is, it is surely something to be avoided. Isn't that the thrust of what He is saying? Avoid being forced to pay what you owe.

> Arrange your matters with those who have anything against you, while you are yet together and things have not gone too far to be arranged; *you will have to do it*, and that under less easy circumstances than now. Putting off is of no use. You must. The thing has to be done; there are means of compelling you. No, there is no escape. There is no heaven with a little of hell in it—no plan to retain this or that of the devil in our hearts or our pockets. Out Satan must go, every hair and feather!

Be they few or many cast into such a prison as I have
endeavored to imagine, there can be no deliverance for
the human soul, whether in that prison or out of it, but in
paying the last farthing, in becoming lowly, penitent, self-
refusing—so receiving the sonship and learning to cry,
Father! . . . God is determined to have his children clean,
clear, pure as very snow. . . .

Payment will be made. All right, if we accept that, what
might we owe others that we should, in Jesus' words, "settle quickly"?

> Fair play (which has nothing to do with how others
> have treated us)
> Unbiased right judgment
> Love for them as for ourselves
> Trust
> Praise that has been withheld
> An opportunity they should have been given
> Rights they have not been given
> Confession of our faults against them
> Prayer for the healing of wounds we have inflicted
> Answers to their questions
> Returned phone calls
> Common politeness
> Believing the best of them
> Forgiveness even if they have not repented
> Respect for them as images of God

God is determined that we make the payment, achieve
the restitution, learn to obey and grow up into "the whole
measure of the fullness of Christ" (Ephesians 4:13). The
attitudes that will most enable us to deal with discipline
are the Lord's own. We, too, must eventually take on and
express love toward others that is patient, kind, keeps no
record of wrongs, and trusts and hopes and perseveres.

All this is to say, giving completes receiving. To fully receive the love God has for us means for us to give love to others. Even Jesus, sinless as He was, had to learn obedience.

Hard Questions About Faith

Number Thirteen: Wasn't it another trick for Jesus to promise that "you may ask me for anything in my name, and I will do it" (John 14:14)? We know He was not writing a blank check, but in context He did not seem to qualify it.

He was "[made] perfect through suffering" (Hebrews 2:10). Sometimes His suffering was to respond to the next person demanding His attention instead of grabbing some much-needed sleep.

Faith is crucial, of course, to successful collaboration with the will of God.

In 1984 my God had the cheek to utter this brief demand to me: *Give up counseling.*

Those three words catapulted me into disbelief, anger, temptation to rebel, confusion and grief, in that order. It did not make sense for me to give up my counseling ministry. I had sat through long seminary courses, read innumerable books, put in untold numbers of hours in counseling and I loved the quality of interaction between myself and those I counseled. Besides, I was pretty good at it.

But I knew I had been told to give it up.

This was one of the times that helped me learn what I have stated earlier in this book: Obedience precedes understanding. I did not learn it quickly. For days I fussed and fumed, trying to make intellectual sense of the command. It just did not compute. What's more, the Lord was silent on *why* I had to give up counseling. The naked command stood there with nothing to support it.

Finally I agreed—reluctantly, petulantly, confusedly. For months I was in a fog as I trained laypersons in the ministry of counseling and turned my counseling ministry over to them. Eventually I came to the point that I no longer had a counseling ministry.

Within weeks I led a small team of parishioners to conduct a conference on power ministry in a neighboring state. It was tremendously successful. Since then (as I have said), I have led more than 130 such conferences, seminars and retreats. I have been blessed to bring numerous churches, denominations, parachurch organizations and individuals into intimate experience with the Holy Spirit in teaching, healing, empowering, discipling and modeling—*none* of which I would have had time for had I continued my counseling ministry!

Gain through Loss

I am getting at a principle that Jesus taught and modeled. I call it "gain through loss." When God asks us to do something costly, it looks like a loss. It *is* a loss. But He is a good God interested only in blessing us. He sees down the road to the gain He will be able to grant us if we obey His invitation to lose the thing He has put His finger on.

What we want to know *for sure*, of course, is that He is the one who has told us. But we have to lay to rest that hope. We do not know for sure but we can know for faith. When we know for faith that He wants us to sacrifice something, we can do it. Obedience is possible. What's more, obedience frees God to give us the thing He envisions for us. What He gives, I have found, is always greater than what He takes.

I enjoy the conference-leading ministry more than I enjoyed counseling. I am better at it than I was at counseling. My gifts and temperament and interests and convictions are all fulfilled more than counseling could ever have done. God knew what He was doing when He told me to give up counseling. I suppose you already know why, when He told me to give it up, He did not tell me the reason. "Without faith it is impossible to please God." You probably already know the reference, too, but here it is again: Hebrews 11:6.

We do not lose in order to gain, but gain is the heaven-inspired consequence of willful obedience. We lose in order to obey. God rewards us in order to bless. Our part is to lose, His to bless. Do not try to figure out *how* God is going to bless you for your willingness to lose. To contemplate the blessing is to compromise the obedience.

"God is determined to have his children clean," wrote MacDonald, "clear, pure as very snow. . . ."

God Himself models this life-losing for us. Let's say you have accepted Jesus Christ into your heart. This has freed God to ascribe Jesus' acceptability to you as a gift. The degree to which the Father accepts Jesus is the degree to which He accepts you. Pretty total, you will agree. But let's say you cling to a particular sin. You confess it when you go to church. It bothers you. You wish you could stop it. But you have not yet stopped. What is the Father's attitude toward you? Does your ongoing sinning endanger His acceptance of you?

Absolutely not. He goes on giving you total acceptance whether you change or not. Does He want you to change? Of course He does. The nature of love is to want the best for the beloved, and that best means change, doesn't it? Is He at work to motivate you to change? Of course. But does that mean He withholds acceptance from you until you change? *No!* He "loses" His life for you. He keeps on forgiving and accepting you whether or not you change one iota. He gives you the reward of change—acceptance—before you change, *and* He manages to work the details of your life so that you are motivated to obey Him.

How does He gain His life? When His acceptance of us, along with His discipline, finally touches our hearts and makes us truly want to change. That kind of wanting seizes the kind of faith that enables change to occur.

I quipped to my congregation one day, "Love the hell out of people. It is the only way the hell goes."

God loves the hell out of us. He keeps on keeping on loving us until we get tired of the hell in us and agree to His plan to change us. When we enter this kind of change, we take our hearts in our hands and present them humbly and thankfully to Him who has loved us with an everlasting love.

This is what He lives for!—the gift of our hearts. When we, in complete free will, take our hearts and give them to Him in motivated gratitude for what He has already done for us, He gets His life back. His love finally comes full-circle and returns to Him from our hearts. What He had lost, He has received and better than before. What we have lost, we have been given. The result is something greater than the sum of its parts—a fullness-in-Him-and-in-us, a fullness impossible to describe unless we link His fullness with ours and ours with His.

The Greek word for fullness, *pleroma*, indicates an exploding synergism, a fullness that gets fuller with each cycle of the givingness of God to man and the return givingness of man to God. What a God! He reserves something of His fullness to a potentiality that can be fulfilled only by our willful collaboration.

Earthen Vessels

The connectedness between God and us, this linkage, this fullness, this sovereign will, this inexorable love, are wonderfully represented in Paul's assertion "We have this treasure in jars of clay [*earthen vessels*, KJV] to show that this all-surpassing power is from God and not from us" (2 Corinthians 4:7).

Christians tend to misrepresent the fullness of this passage by focusing on the treasure at the expense of the earthen vessel, or on the vessel at the expense of the treasure.

Some focus exclusively on the grandeur, holiness and glory of God, little esteeming the human vessel designed to contain God. God is great, they say; man is nothing. This works out in practice to covering or camouflaging or hiding or denying the weaknesses of human nature. These Christians are sublimating human nature in favor of the flawless nature of God. You walk on eggshells around them because you might reveal some unacceptable expression of humanity in yourself or touch off one in them.

Other Christians focus so completely on *their* growth, *their* holiness, *their* healing, *their* everything that they give little or no attention to the divine treasure in them. These persons regard God almost as a static, impersonal resource to be tapped for their own advancement.

According to the fullness of Christianity, however, we have this treasure *in* earthen vessels. Watchman Nee makes the point well:

> This is possibly the clearest statement there is of the nature of practical Christianity. Christianity is not the earthen vessel, nor is it the treasure, but it is *the treasure in the earthen vessel.*

The Paul who called us earthen vessels shared openly that he was sorrowful, had shed many tears, was perplexed, had even despaired. He was a man who was afraid yet determined; surrounded by foes yet not bound; about to be overcome yet not destroyed; weak yet strong.

"My grace is sufficient for you," Jesus said to him, "for my power is made perfect in weakness" (2 Corinthians 12:9). Jesus Himself claims that the perfection of His power depends on the weakness of the vessel in whom it is revealed. Without human weakness to contain it, divine power is not manifested. It is no good shouting down the human in order to lift up the divine or ignoring the divine to lift up the human. The treasure apart from the vessel is not to be treasured. The vessel apart from the treasure is not ultimately treasureable.

For a long time I expected that if I got enough teaching, enough grace, enough healing or enough conviction, I would rise to a level of untemptability, especially with regard to my besetting sins. Can you identify with that? I thought it would give God glory if I got to the place where I was past being tempted in these areas. Immunity, I thought, must be the definition of victory.

Into the long record of innumerable skirmishes with temptation came a resolution of sorts. Not the one I had expected nor the one I had hoped for. I had wanted something finalized. What I got was the finalized One who is making Himself available to and in me moment by moment for the purpose of displaying (among other qualities) His resistance to temptation.

It is walking persistently on the edge of the precipice. I am not always on the edge, of course, but I am there often enough to realize that there is no permanent escape from it. God is the One who keeps me returning to it, so that He can reveal the priceless treasure of His temptation-repulsing life *in me*.

What did Paul state is the hope of glory? Is it Christ? No. Us? No. It is "*Christ in you*, the hope of glory" (Colossians 1:27). God has authored a reality wherein His own glory refuses to come into fullness unless it is displayed in us. Even Jesus in His humanity modeled this divinity-displaying weakness, asserting over and over that He was impotent without the immediate help of the Father. He freely displayed the weakness of His fear in Gethsemane, of His vulnerability in court, of His physical limitations along the Via Dolorosa, of His spiritual strength in hanging naked on a cross. As Paul summarized, "To be sure, he was crucified in weakness, yet he lives by God's power" (2 Corinthians 13:4).

There it is again, that incredible *yet!* Weak yet strong, crucified yet raised, dead yet alive.

Paul goes right on to apply that *yet* to us: "Likewise, we are weak in him, yet by God's power we will live with Him to serve you" (13:4). Then he exhorts his hearers to conduct a test: "Examine yourselves to see whether you are in the faith; test yourselves. Do you not realize that Christ Jesus is in you—unless, of course, you fail the test?" (13:5). The answer to the test is that Christ Jesus *is* in you. That is what it means to have faith, to be spiritually alive. That is the treasure in the vessel.

"Even my grasp on Jesus is weak," Paul was saying. "We are weak in Him." Yet . . . yet what? Yet I am growing better and better every day in every way? Yet I am defeating the enemy as I rise above his enticements? No. "Yet by God's power we will live with him." We are radically dependent on God for the consistent, moment-by-moment deployment of His life and power in us. That dependence gives Him glory.

What did Paul conclude about his weaknesses? Bless his soul, he *boasted* about them!

> Therefore I will boast all the more gladly about my weaknesses, so that Christ's power may rest on me. That is why, for Christ's sake, I delight in weaknesses, in insults, in hardships, in persecutions, in difficulties. For when I am weak, then I am strong.
>
> 2 Corinthians 12:9–10

Paul did not try to outgrow his weaknesses or blowtorch them out of his soul. He boasted about them because they demonstrated the treasure in the earthen vessel.

The inexorable love of God is wooing your sovereign will to respond into the fullness-escalating intimacy of Him-in-you. He respects you utterly and will approach you in discipline and in love, in truth and in mercy, in patience and in urgency, all in order to appeal to the sovereignty of your will.

What point of contention lies between you and Him at the moment? You are the judge. What is your decision?

13
A Final Exhortation

As I cast my eye back over the ground we have covered in this book, I find that my heart wants to urge you to "Go for it!" in this business of having faith. My attention lands on one last Greek word—the word for *exhortation, paraklesis*. It does not mean a stern lecture or strong goading or condemning finger under the nose. The word literally means "a calling alongside." *Exhortation* is a gentle word conveying a happy partnership.

It would be lovely to be called alongside *you* in order to walk with you in your business of having faith. Let me do this for a moment in these pages as I think back to the first verse we looked at: "When the Son of Man comes, will he find faith on the earth?" (Luke 18:8). I would like to conclude this book by looking forward to that day, trying to imagine what it will be like.

Scripture tells us that none of us knows when that day is going to occur, that it will be a surprise, that it will occur suddenly and that everyone will recognize Jesus instantly as the King of the universe. After the shock and joy of His arrival and you know it is really He and that you are in His private presence, I can imagine that He would say,

Child, let's look at your life and see how your faith has managed.

Child, I want to tell you how happy I am that you've been walking in consistent faith. Your faith has pleased almighty God. You've been growing, experimenting in the modes of faith to which teachings have exposed you. You have a backlog of faithful episodes to present to Me as a gift.

I am especially glad that you have experimented with the exercise of your will. I am gratified to find that you were set free from mistaken notions about faith and have been encouraged to walk in willful faith, understanding the role your faculties were meant to play in collaboration with Me.

I am pleased that you have experimented freely in various methods of having faith, and especially that you found certain ones that worked well for you.

It is enormously satisfying to Me that you have effectively counteracted the enemies of your faith and have not permitted them to sidetrack you. I find you "in but not of the world," proficient in your refutation

- *of cultural blockages to faith,*
- *of Satan's devices and attacks on you,*
- *of misapplied Christian teaching,*
- *of false ideas of doubt,*
- *and of the ungodly inclination to go it alone.*

The nerve endings of My soul tingle with joy because you have taken courage and acted boldly in the gift of faith that My Spirit made available to you from time to time.

I find that you have been guarding and expanding your freedom in Me, and I am immensely gratified with this appreciation of My sacrifice for you.

As I look over your life, My child, I notice that you have frequently bent your will to conform to Mine, and this propels My joy beyond bounds because I am now able to invite you into greatness, saying, "Come, you who are blessed by my Father; take your inheritance, the kingdom prepared for you since the creation of the world" (Matthew 25:34).

As I look for and find faith in you, I find My own character represented in your attitudes, priorities and actions.

As I look for and find faith in you, I find that others have been helped, healed, given to, taught, guided or befriended by you.

As I look for and find faith in you, I find that others have been encouraged to believe for themselves in the wake of your example.

As I look for and find faith in you, I find that society has been influenced for good on large and small fields.

As I look for and find faith in you, I find that My own promises to you have been fulfilled, setting My Lover's heart free to rejoice in the benefits I've given you, My beloved.

Well, I come alongside you now to encourage you that you can hear these commendations coming to you from the mouth of your Lord. You *can* believe, you *can* exercise effective faith because He is here to help you do it. If you are not believing as you should, He will gladly help you believe as you should. Believe *that!*

The bottom line: Trust God. That is all these teachings have been designed for, by identifying blockages and offering a few morsels of advice—to help you trust God. Go for it! Go for it for the rest of your life. This is your only chance to have faith and to prove that faith works. When you get to heaven, you will not need faith anymore, for you will have Him who takes the place of faith.

So trust Him now.

Sources Used and Recommended

Barclay, William. *The Letters to the Corinthians*. Philadelphia: The Westminster Press, 1975.

Carpenter, Humphrey. *The Inklings*. Boston: Houghton Mifflin Co., 1979.

Cowman, Mrs. Charles E. *Streams in the Desert*. Vol. 2. Grand Rapids: Zondervan, 1966.

DeArteaga, William. *Quenching the Spirit*. Lake Mary, Fla.: Creation House, 1992.

Edman, V. Raymond. *They Found the Secret*. Grand Rapids: Zondervan, 1960.

Flynn, Mike. *Holy Vulnerability*. Grand Rapids: Chosen Books, 1990.

Flynn, Mike, and Doug Gregg. *Inner Healing*. Downers Grove: InterVarsity Press, 1993.

Grubb, Norman. *Touching the Invisible*. Ft. Washington, Pa.: Christian Literature Crusade, 1978.

Keirsey, David, and Marilyn Bates. *Please Understand Me*. Del Mar, Calif.: Prometheus Nemesis Books, 1978.

Lawrence, Brother. *The Practice of the Presence of God.* White Plains, N.Y.: Peter Pauper Press, Inc., 1963.

Lewis, C. S. *Christian Reflections.* Edited by Walter Hooper. Grand Rapids: Eerdmans, 1967.

MacDonald, George. *Life Essential.* Wheaton: Harold Shaw Publishers, 1974.

MacDonald, George. *Unspoken Sermons.* 3 vols. Eureka, Calif.: Sunrise Books, Publishers, 1989.

Nee, Watchman. *What Shall This Man Do?* Ft. Washington, Pa.: Christian Literature Crusade, 1961.

Phillips, Michael R. *George MacDonald.* Minneapolis: Bethany House Publishers, 1987.

Tittmann, George F. *What Manner of Love.* New York: Morehouse-Barlow Co., 1959.

Vine, W. E. *An Expository Dictionary of New Testament Words.* Grand Rapids: Fleming H. Revell, 1966.

White, John. *Eros Redeemed.* Downers Grove: InterVarsity Press, 1993.

Williams, Charles. *War in Heaven.* Grand Rapids: Eerdmans, 1949.